IDLE THOUGHTS

& OTHER STUFF

JACK IDLE

**Grosvenor House
Publishing Limited**

The right of Jack Idle to be identified as the author of this
work has been asserted in accordance with Section 78
of the Copyright, Designs and Patents Act 1988

The book cover picture is copyright to Jack Idle

This book is published by
Grosvenor House Publishing Ltd
Link House
140 The Broadway, Tolworth, Surrey, KT6 7HT.
www.grosvenorhousepublishing.co.uk

A CIP record for this book
is available from the British Library

ISBN 978-1-78623-221-2

CONTENTS

INTRODUCTION v

IDLE THOUGHTS AND OTHER STUFF 1

ACKNOWLEDGEMENTS 144

INDEX 145

ABOUT THE AUTHOR 146

INTRODUCTION

This book is dedicated to my friend Jack Ware whose last request was to tell him another one.

It is mostly a collection of stuff that came my way, or I made up, that made us both smile, chuckle or laugh out loud, with occasional serious observations on life today.

Much of the humour is old but timeless, from authors and comedians, some of whom are long dead, but whose wit lives on, having been adapted to suit new audiences. Doubtless, some of it will date and fade from our memories, along with its targets hopefully.

My own contributions have been inspired by many of those duly acknowledged at the end of the book, and I apologise for any oversights. It may be freely repeated without fear of copyright infringement, so please do so.

Unfortunately, today much of the material many of us still find humorous will be branded politically incorrect – sexist, racist etc. I don't care, because for myself none of it has that intent, and I have been even-handed, mocking as many as I can, myself included. Some of it is naughty, occasionally very naughty without being too explicit or offensive, and mild vernacular language has only been retained when important to its context.

The book would have been in colour but I couldn't find my crayons.

There is not a shred of evidence that life is serious.

Ogden Nash.

Every day, I sit down in a chair that isn't there, but that's the story of my life.

I move in high circles, and not just those over Heathrow.

My three sisters gave me dancing lessons each morning outside the bathroom.

Old people are only grey on the outside.

I think my watch has stopped, either that or I have died.

When you die, it's a problem for the people around you. It's the same when you are stupid.

In these politically heated and polarised times, I am planning an escape to somewhere more temperate, like Antarctica.

Give a man a fish and he will be fed for the day.
Teach a man to fish and he will likely disappear for the weekend.

Nowadays, muggers are so much more sophisticated. Yesterday, I was in the bank and a well-dressed young man sat me down and without any hint of aggression said, "Can I interest you in some life insurance?"

America was the first nation to put a man on the Moon, and, less than fifty years later, to establish the first Idiocracy.

———————

An article in New Scientist suggests that a small nuclear war could reverse the effects of global warming. That sounds a lot easier than sorting my waste into those coloured bins.

———————

Last summer when my air conditioner broke down, I solved the problem by leaving the fridge door open.

———————

Absence is always the best defence.

———————

He could read her like a book in braille that no publisher would dare touch.

———————

If women are truly uncomfortable with men staring at their chests, they could stop wearing those ridiculously high heels.

———————

Even when people are avoiding you, you should still look both ways when crossing the road.

———————

"Watson, I wonder why Mrs. Hudson isn't answering the door."
"Perhaps she's entertaining, Holmes."
"Really, Watson, I've never found her so."

COMMUNICATION BREAKDOWN 1

Paddy is in a steaming rage packing his suitcase when his mother-in-law arrives.

"What's happened, Paddy?" she asks anxiously.

"What's happened? I'll tell you what's happened! I sent an email to my wife, your daughter, telling her I'd finished my assignment ahead of time, and was coming home a day early. I get home and guess what I find? Your daughter, my wife, naked in our marital bed with Joe Murphy! This is unforgivable, the end of the marriage, I'm done, I'm leaving."

"Calm down, Paddy!" says his mother-in-law. "This is all very odd. I can't believe she would ever do such a thing. There has to be a simple explanation, so let me speak to her immediately and find out what's happened."

Minutes later, she returns with a big smile, "Paddy, I told you it's all a simple misunderstanding and none of it's her fault. She never got your email."

———

No one can project such darkness as he who has seen the light.

———

Women pursuing equality in the workplace can be easily recognised by their make-up and shoes.

———

The one-eyed dinosaur was called Idontincisaurus.

HOLIDAY HEAVEN

Two priests went to the French Riviera for a relaxing break. As soon as the plane landed they headed for the beach store and bought outrageous shorts, sandals and sunhats, so they would not be recognised as clergy.

Next morning, they were on the beach, enjoying their drinks, sunshine and the sights when a topless beauty strolled past, smiled rather coyly and said, "Good morning, Father, good morning, Father."

Stunned, they looked each other up and down, and wondered how she knew they were priests. So back to the store they went to buy a couple of very silly beach shirts and returned to their chairs to relax in the sunshine once more.

Later in the day, the same beauty passed them, and again she nodded at each of them saying "Good afternoon, Father, good afternoon, Father."

The elder priest was so surprised he blurted out, "Young lady, how on earth do you know we are priests, dressed like this?"

"Well," she replied, "if you look me in the eye, you'll see it's me, Sister Mary."

Generally speaking, there are always two types of people – those who do, and those who don't.

A man walks into a pub with a lump of tarmac under his arm, and says to the landlord, "A pint for me, and one for the road."

Drinker: "This looks like a 'men only' bar; don't you serve women?"
Landlord: "No, you have to bring your own."

Landlord: "Look Shakey, I told you after that drunken brawl last week with your Italian pals, you're bard."

Don't kick a man when he is down, just in case he stirs.

In a smart man's hands, a woman will be putty.

But the other way around, the opposite occurs.

Police advised me to extend my home security system, so I fitted a motion detector in the lavatory.

Only twelve shoplifting days till Christmas!

(Liverpool greeting)

I was the last one of eight children before my mother sewed up that hole in father's pyjamas. Hence the saying, a stitch in time...

THE INTRUDER

A man misses his train and gets home in the early hours to be confronted by his tearful wife.

Act 1.

Man: "What's happened?"
Wife: "Well, when you didn't arrive home, I had supper alone, went to bed, read for a while, turned out the light and fell asleep …"
Man: "And?"
Wife: "Then a man broke in, rummaged around downstairs, came upstairs and started to …"
Man: "But, did he take anything, or did he leave empty-handed?"
Wife: "Empty-handed, but I thought it was you, so he did take quite a few liberties."

Act 2.

Police Inspector: "So, madam, you say that physically the man resembled your husband. But what was it exactly that made you suspicious it wasn't him."

Wife: "Three things actually: his splendid enthusiasm, his technical expertise and his remarkable stamina."

Police Inspector: "Hmm, I was thinking something more tangible, more useful in a conventional line up."

Wife: "Well, if you are very quick, the scratches on his buttocks."

Act 3.

Police Inspector: "Good news, madam, we have apprehended your intruder, but since he didn't steal anything, we aren't sure what to charge him with. If we charge him with assault, he's likely to get a five-year custodial sentence, less time off for good behaviour, or if the Judge is inclined to leniency and there are no objections from the victim, perhaps a period of community service."

Wife: "Well, that would be perfect, if I could have him five hours, five nights a week for the next five years."

_____

"Doctor, I need some sleeping tablets for my husband."
"What's his problem?"
"He's woken up."

_____

Fortunately, the future of mankind is only a brief phenomenon.

_____

Woman: "Stop the coach, please, driver; you've left my husband behind."
Driver: "Don't worry, I'm sure there'll be another one along shortly."

_____

This morning I was awoken by heavy breathing next to me, but it was only the wife's 'Darth Vader' ringtone.

One problem with alcohol is that it encourages ugly people to multiply.

―――――――

Women may be hard to live with, but without them men would be buggered.

―――――――

It's odd that women protest about sexual harassment and groping <u>and</u> being refused entry to 'men-only' clubs.

―――――――

I hope I'm never old enough to know better.

―――――――

My wife is the exact double of Kate Moss. That's an amazing 224lbs.

―――――――

~~I think therefore I drink.~~
~~I drink therefore I am.~~
~~I am therefore I drink.~~
~~I drink therefore I think.~~
~~I am therefore I think.~~

I think therefore I am.

René Descartes

―――――――

Manliness is the freedom to do whatever you want, wherever you want, and how you want when the coast is clear.

At 80 years of age I'm still a sex icon, but only for those who don't care anymore.

It's a relief that human nature is not regarded as part of our culture.

When gripped by uncertainty or tiredness, I find an ambitious beauty will often stiffen my resolve.

BBC FUTURE BROKEN NEWS

IKEA have been forced to abandon their new drone delivery service after two drones collided over west London today.

One man almost suffocated under a comfy sofa after refusing to get up, whilst another also had a lucky escape when he was trapped inside a wardrobe for several hours without food or beer, until his wife read him the assembly instructions backwards.

His reaction was disbelief, "I couldn't believe my luck, a fully assembled flat-pack out of the blue. A few feet further over and it could have been curtains for the wife."

Hillingdon Council have fined IKEA for their unauthorised additions to local street furniture.
A council spokes said, "We cannot take this sort of incident lying down, unless it's a top of the range double bed."

A big advantage of being short is that the views can be more rewarding.

_____

Junk is what you keep in your shed for years and throw out, just before you find a need for it.

_____

Man created God in his own image.

_____

His modesty demanded he should stand last in line, even when he was alone.

_____

My life has been a lesson in how to lose gracefully.

_____

My neighbour always has a friendly word too many.

_____

If you weigh 100kg you are overweight, although on Mars that would only be 38kg.

It might be easier to forget the diet and move there.

_____

It's not true that men can't concentrate on more than one thing at a time. Every woman I know has two breasts.

_____

I wonder if clouds ever look down at us and think, 'That one looks like an idiot.'

My dyslexic dog thinks he's omnipotent.

———————

I never wear shorts in mixed company in case they fail to cover my enthusiasm.

———————

If you owe the bank a million and can't pay it back, you've got a problem. If you owe them ten million, they've got the problem.

———————

Men can shout each other down to get their point over, but they can never talk over a woman.

———————

He had a remarkable ability for defeating everyone's expectations.

———————

Old Dear 1: "Isn't it windy today?"
Old Dear 2: "No, I'm sure it's Thursday."
Old Dear 3: "Me too."
Old Dear 4: "Doubles all round then, please Waiter."

———————

Barman: "I've never seen a dog in here playing chess with his owner before. He must be very smart."

Customer: "I'm afraid not, four moves and it's check every time."

———————

We were so poor we only lived in black and white.

However hard he pressed, he never managed to achieve a deeper relationship with her.

————————

PROVIDENCE

Sitting at her window in the convent, Sister Mary opened a letter from home.

Inside was a £50 note that her parents had sent with a message to spend it with love. Sister Mary smiled at their kindness, while simultaneously noticing a shabbily dressed old man in the cold street below leaning against a lamppost for warmth.

Quickly she wrote, "Don't despair – Sister Mary" on some notepaper, wrapped the £50 note in it, opened the window and threw it down to him.

The old man picked it up, and with a smile, a wave and a tip of his hat, went off down the street and disappeared into the local betting shop.

"Oh well," she thought, "if that makes him happy, so be it, it's not for me to judge him."

The next day, Sister Mary was called to the front door to see a visitor. She went down and found the same shabbily dressed old man standing there. Without a word, he handed her a huge wad of £50 notes. "What's this?" she asked.

"Yours, Sister," he replied, "Don't Despair came in at 100/1."

——

Following her unexpected windfall, Sister Mary ponders her options:

- She distributes the money amongst the poor.
- She opens a soup kitchen.
- She buys a lifetime subscription to Racing Gazette.

The chicken crossed the road just because it was in a fowl mood.

If you arrive home late from a night out with the boys, and are met by the wife standing on the doorstep with a broom in her hands, avoid the smart alec remark such as, "Still doing the housework or are you flying off somewhere?"

And if you have perfume or lipstick on your collar, avoid the wink and slap on the bottom, saying, "You're next, Chubby."

Myth 1: Jesus was literally the Son of God.

I have come to the conclusion that Guy Fawkes was a man well ahead of his time.

It wasn't until Jack was thirty-five that he discovered the term 'bloody architect' was two separate words.

A man lost his dog and put an advert in the local paper that read, "Here, boy!"

I have long suspected that Jack and the Beanstalk is just another tall story.

I have set my personal goals so high, it is pointless striving to attain them.

My command of the English language is so complete that everyone knows it is them that there is something wrong with.

I see the price of Viagra is also going up.

Nowadays, a man should never approach a woman unless she has already slipped her monogrammed scanties with a signed letter of authorisation into his jacket pocket.

Solitude is preferable to the company of inferior people.

I love the sound of church bells on Sunday mornings even if it is the vicar selling his ice-cream.

Unfortunately, life is full of pleasures that often cancel each other out.

It's the small, simple things in life that make it so meaningless.

———————

I persuaded my wife to change her name to Alexa, hoping she'd do as she was told.

It didn't work but at least she listens to me, sometimes.

———————

Pollution in London is now so bad the RSPB has released a CD of bird coughs.

———————

I know lots of famous people, and they always greet me with, 'And who are you?'

———————

A true friend loves you even when you succeed.

———————

Policeman: "You do not have to say anything, but it may harm your defence if you do not mention when questioned something which you later rely on in court. Anything you do say may be given in evidence and used against you."

Man: "I know; I'm married."

———————

Marriage is not only a word but also a sentence, with no time off for good behaviour.

———————

We were so poor we could only afford nick names.

I don't understand why my wife wastes so much time trying to make me look stupid.

———

Her female intuition is so highly developed, she knows I am wrong before I even open my mouth.

———

I don't understand why women cover themselves in all that ridiculous make-up, and then complain men never take them seriously.

———

I started wearing women's underwear after my wife found some under the passenger seat.

———

I watched *Swimming with Sharks* last night on Netflix. Not only were there no sharks but no Kevin Spacey either.

———

I offered my Gary Glitter CDs on eBay, but they told me nobody would *wanna touch* them.

———

Time, tide and dirty dishes wait for no man.

———

My wife was disappointed she couldn't find the expensive Christmas present she wanted for me.

I told her that it didn't matter as I'd be more than happy with any cheap stocking filler.

BBC BROKEN NEWS: SEXUAL HARASSMENT LATEST

In the wake of the harassment scandal that has whetted people's appetites around UK, the PM is seeking cross party agreement for a revolutionary reorganisation of the Commons.

The plan is to abandon the traditional party bench arrangement, in favour of a true 'free for all' set-up that would allow MPs to sit wherever he or she wanted. This is believed might encourage a cross-fertilisation of political ideas and a more consensual parliamentary life in general.

A vocal opposition group, dubbed the 'Puritans', is pressing for maintaining the current arrangement, but with a more radical division into 'predators and vestal virgins'.

At the end of tonight's late session, MPs will be expected to reveal their inclinations with a show of both hands.

———

Theresa May is to impose a new dress code in Parliament – padlocked codpieces and burkas.

———

It is ironic that MPs still address each other as Honourable Member.

———————

Politicians are always there when they want your vote.

Christmas shopping is just too long and tedious.
I much preferred it when it all happened on Christmas
Eve, on Fifth Avenue, in black and white.

———————————

Kim Jong Un: "I have a nuclear button on my desk."
Donald Trump: "So do I, and it's better than yours."
Kim Jong Un: "But my dick is bigger than yours."
Donald Trump: "Oh no, it isn't."
Kim Jong Un: "Oh yes, it is."
Donald Trump: "Oh no, it isn't."
etc., etc.

———————————

After he's done Europe, Santa Claus might want to stay
out of US airspace.

———————————

I've cured my cash allergy by having my pension paid
directly into my Amazon Wine account.

———————————

Women come in all shapes and sizes but are much
easier to get the measure of when lying down.

———————————

The nearest thing to paradise is a good obituary.

———————————

I am of the opinion that by and large, women are very
opinionated.

———————————

His desire to be loved was so strong that everyone hated
him.

Irony is the state that those who have the least to say have the largest audiences.

———————

I bought some of that old-fashioned vanishing cream for the wife, but she is still here.

———

The cream has vanished though.

———————

If you find symmetry attractive, by all means turn the other cheek.

———————

Myth 2: Christopher Columbus discovered North America.

———————

The man in the street is easily run over by the Clapham omnibus.

———————

Love will bloom under cultivation, but hate is a weed that grows on its own.

———————

Without his family behind him he would never have been encouraged to commit so much of his time at his work.

———————

You only have one chance to make a good last impression.

———————

The middle class is just a two-faced buffer zone.

———————

Myth 3: Democracy is the exercising of your rights.

———————

He was so small and ugly that people generously described him as gifted.

I was so small and ugly my parents left home.

———————

Without language it would be impossible to talk ourselves into or out of trouble.

———————

The shroud was his final fashion statement.

———————

His obituary outshone everything he had ever written.

———————

I love the aerodynamic shape of women and the heights they can reach when excited, though not when they fly off the handle.

———

Speaking of which, that expression's association with women surely has something to do with broomsticks.

———

And speaking of aerodynamics, a man's raised undercarriage often results in some very uncomfortable landings.

I like to see women exceeding expectations in the workplace, and for that matter in the kitchen and bedroom too.

I once had a girlfriend who had no maternal instincts whatsoever, which I found unbearable, inconceivable, and quite impregnable.

Feminism has nothing to do with femininity.

Everybody seems to be expert in solving other people's problems.

It's absurd that the word 'monosyllabic' should have more than one.

Your schooldays may be the best time of your life, but they are only the beginning of the sentence.

Narcissists should never marry, especially each other.

Myth 4: Global warming can be reduced or reversed without us reducing our energy consumption.

We were so poor we lived in an empty coal shed for warmth.

TELEPHONE BANKING

Clerk: "Before we discuss your account, I need to go through some security questions with you. Can you identify yourself please?"

Me: "Yes, when I got out of bed this morning and saw myself in the bathroom mirror, I recognized myself instantly."

Clerk: "Excellent, and how old will you be on your next birthday?"

Me: "Well, if I'm 81 now, then I guess 82, if I ever make it beyond this phone call."

Clerk: "Correct, and can you confirm your address for me, please."

Me: "Yes, I still live at home."

Clerk: "Excellent, and can you tell me how many sugars you take in your tea?"

Me: "Can I pass you over to my wife to answer that one, please?"

———————

God doesn't play dice, simply because the odds would still be 5 to 1 against Him.

———————

His future stood there before him like a mountain of impossibilities.

Scoundrels are always charming and sociable.

———————

She felt so overlooked everyone noticed it.
And the certainty that she wasn't needed made her stay.

———————

The trousers were so tight that sexual contact was
superfluous.

———————

The secrets she took to her grave were soon forgotten.

———————

The chicken crossed the road, so it wouldn't be seen
dead in KFC.

———————

It wasn't until I opened the wrong end of my chocolate-
coated gingers that I saw the desperate message on the
undersides,

"Help, I'm a prisoner in a biscuit factory."

———————

Love thy neighbour, but keep the fence well maintained.

———————

I have faced many a tough battle armed only with a knife
and fork.

———————

His terminal illness coincided with that brief religious
period in his life.

A WHIFF OF REVENGE

Jack was distraught at the failure of his marriage through no fault of his own.

On the first day after the divorce, he sadly packed his personal belongings into boxes, suitcases and plastic bags.

On the second day, he had the removal company come and collect them.

On the third day, he sat down for the last time at their beautiful dining room table. He played her favourite music, and enjoyed her favourite food – shrimp, caviar, a bottle of champagne – and oddly, three tins of sardines. When he had finished, he went into every room and stuffed the leftovers into the hollow centres of the curtain rods. Then, he cleaned up the kitchen and left.

On the fourth day, his ex-wife returned with her new boyfriend, and at first all was bliss.

Then slowly, the house began to smell, and then stink. They tried everything including professional deep cleaning. Floorboards were lifted to check for dead rodents, and carpets were steam-cleaned.
The house was repainted inside and out.
Air fresheners were hung everywhere.
Exterminators were brought in to fumigate the place, during which time they had to move out.
In the end they even replaced the carpets, but nothing worked.

Their friends stopped coming to visit them.
Repairmen refused to work in the house.
Finally, they couldn't take the stench any longer, and decided they had to sell up and move on.

Months later, even though they'd reduced the price by half, they couldn't find a buyer.

Finally, unable to wait any longer, they took a loan from the bank and bought a new place.

A few days later, Jack called his ex-wife and asked how things were going.
She told him about her impending move, and that she needed to sell the house to escape her marriage ghosts.
He listened politely and said that if she would be willing to reduce her divorce settlement, he would buy the house from her at market valuation.
In desperation, she agreed on a price that was only a fraction of what the house had been worth, and within two hours her solicitors delivered the completed paperwork.

The next day, his ex-wife and her boyfriend smiled in relief as they watched the removal company pack all their belongings to take to their new home.

And to spite her ex-husband, they took the door keys, toilet rolls, light bulbs and the curtain rods...

———————

His life was such a puzzle he wondered what the catch was.

The key difference between a fortress and a prison is one's state of mind, and the location of the key.

His love for humanity demanded its full and undivided attention.

He saw the light at the end of the tunnel, just before the train hit him, from behind.

Man: "Since it's my birthday, do you fancy trying something from the Kama Sutra?"

Wife: "Let's be really bold and have the Chicken Biryani."

Man: "Since it's your birthday, do you fancy trying something from the Kama Sutra?"

Wife: "That dishy waiter looks rather athletic."

Man: "You are my best friend, and I really love you."
Wife: "Is that you or the wine talking now?"
Man: "Sorry, I was talking to the wine."

The most interesting women always have a past.

BBC BROKEN NEWS: SEXUAL HARASSMENT GRIPS UK AGAIN

Scotland Yard has launched a nationwide woman-hunt after allegations of sexual harassment made by an 80-year-old male singer, who was awarded an OBE in 1999 and knighted in 2006, but who has exercised his right to anonymity under UK law.

The offences go back over 50 years when women totally unknown to him would routinely scream sexual innuendo at him and shower him with their underwear whilst he was performing in public. The police are now pawing through a mountain of evidence that had been retained by the singer, and plan to conduct door to drawer enquiries in their attempts to match them to their previous occupants, a task that has been made almost impossible by the passage of time, failing memories and middle age spread.

A police spokesman confirmed that they would scrutinise the evidence and all suspects until the culprits had been identified and fitted up, and any attempted cover-ups of past indiscretions would also be exposed for further public humiliation.

———

In the House of Commons today, the PM said she had never attended any of his concerts, and never worn monogrammed scanties.

———————

Trish: "Is there anything else I can get you, dear?"
Jack: "Maybe just a little excited?"

Patient: "Doctor, look at my hands, they're shaking badly."
Doctor: "I have warned you before to cut down on your drinking."
Patient: "I have, Doctor, most of it ends up on the floor."

Bob: "Do you fancy Hawaii for our anniversary?"

Ann: "That's so romantic, but where will you go?"

Caesar adsum iam forte,
Brutus adurat,
Caesar sic in omnibus,
Brutus ini sat.

My local supermarket is offering used trolleys for £1 each. I'm doing a roaring trade on eBay, and I've still got my original investment.

£1 for a trolley is better value than 20 plastic bags at 5p each, and easier to take home.

Myth 5: CCTV is there for your security.

I stopped writing jokes for Jimmy Carr because he wasn't very funny.

Gratitude may be in the dictionary but rarely in life.

My wife and I have started seeing other people since we left the opticians.

Hi Tony

After the Xmas party, I found a bag containing some blank Christmas cards and a toy catapult with foam bullets. I don't suppose it belongs to you?

Mxx

Hi Mel

If there's an AK47, a bag of fertiliser and a timing device in it as well, it's not mine.

Txxx

Man: "Am I the first man to make love to you?"
Woman: "What did you say your name was?"

This year's school play is Shakespeare's *Hamlet*.

All parents and pupils are invited to come and see this tragic performance.

I thought my girlfriend's weight training was aimed at a trimmer figure, until I saw her 100lb snatch.

Interviewer: "Where do you live at present?"

Interviewee: "Liverpool."

Interviewer: "Is that all your life?"

Interviewee: "Well, I'm only 35, so I hope not."

―――――――――

Shopper: "A box of 200 brass screws, please."

Assistant: "How long do you want them?"

Shopper: "Well, once I'd paid for them, I was rather hoping to keep them."

―――――――――

It was the clergyman's knee that cured any further interest in religion.

―――――――――

Cannibal: "I thought that clown tasted a little funny?"

Wife: "He'd have been better with a bit more sauce."

―――――――――

Watson: "Holmes, look up at the sky and tell me what you deduce from your observations."

Holmes: "I see thousands upon thousands of stars which, astronomically, leads me to the view that there are thousands if not millions of planets out there. Astrologically, I see that Saturn is in Leo, and meteorologically, the clear sky suggests that tomorrow will be fine with some light showers later in the day. What about you, Watson?"

Watson: "I reckon someone has stolen the tent."

―――――――――

Myth 6: Cycle lanes improve traffic conditions.

Man: "Here you are, Cabby, £20 including a tip."
Cabby: "Thanks, but the fare is £25."
Man: "And the tip is 'next time take the £20 route'."

———————

A BRIEF CV

Child prodigy, artist, designer, architect, planner, expert in generalities, astronomer, cosmologist, free-thinker, philosopher, visionary, and prophet of doom.

———————

Jews are very good at suffering and finding the best bagels in town.

———————

In every man there is a shed trying to break out and imprison him.

———————

After I got rid of my embarrassing rash, 35 out of 37 women agreed it was a splendid improvement.

One told me to put my trousers back on, and the other reported me to my probation officer.

———————

After God failed to deliver a bicycle for my birthday, I stole one and prayed for His forgiveness instead.

———————

You know when a woman has left the straight and narrow by the trail of male prospectors in her wake.

———————

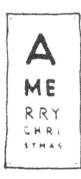

The philosopher is a blind man stumbling around in a dark cellar at night looking for a black cat that isn't there.

The theologian is the man who finds it.

———————

The Shona language has no word for 'unbreakable'.

———————

When I was sixteen my father found an unopened pack of condoms in my pocket, and confronting me said, "There are two possibilities, one, you're showing off to your pals, or two, you hope to get lucky. Which is it?"

"The former," I replied, which ironically also turned out to be the latter.

———————

Absolutely nothing in existence is idiot-proof.

———————

If you want to be remembered after you are gone, leave some unpaid bills.

———————

When you clean something, you are only making something else dirty.

———————

From our European perspective the Wild West still starts at New York.

———————

If God made the world, why did he bother making urinals?

Maybe oxygen is a poison that takes around 70 years to work.

———————

Myth 7: Airport Security has made flying safer.

———————

The trouble with life is that it is just one damned thing after another.

The trouble with death is that you miss life's punchline.

Perhaps death is life's punchline.

———————

One should always remain sceptical, at least until the official denial.

———————

When my friend and her daughter come to stay, I have to get in extra supplies. They are the only people I know who at a single sitting can get through a whole roll of paper.

———————

In response to criticism of the disproportionately low appearance of racial minorities on television, the BBC is to resurrect an extended version of *Crimewatch*.

———————

"Far away is close at hand in images of elsewhere."

———————

We were so poor I thought a slice of bread was called a sandwich.

I bought a book on speed-reading, but never had time to read it.

———

I finally went on a speed-reading course and read *War and Peace* in twenty minutes. It's about Russia.

———

Last night, the lazy waiter asked me for a tip.
So I gave him one, "Ascot, 2:30, 'You Must Be Joking'."

———

The airport security experience primarily consists of pat-downs, serial unzipping, enthusiastic rummaging to uncover illicit goodies or naughties, and the invariable disappointment in their absence.

A bit like my sex life.

———

Sex: The activity is ridiculous, the pleasure momentary, and the consequences can last a lifetime.

———

As a child, I found my Uncle Dick and Aunt Fanny very entertaining, especially through the keyhole.

———

Give me an older woman who knows what's what, anytime please.

———

I had a dozen oysters last night but only half of them worked.

My teenage son bought a car so that he can pursue his career as a mobile sperm bank.

Nowadays, my close encounters are only at airport security.

As a child, I remember the first time that strawberries and ice cream appeared on the kitchen table in front of me. "Yippee", I exclaimed.
"Would you like the same again tomorrow?" my mother asked, and at the same time as I replied, "Yes, please", the bowl disappeared back into the fridge.

To start the day, mother always said, you can't beat a hard-boiled egg.

My wife claims she has an egg allergy, but oddly she appears to be immune to cakes.

A UCLA statistical study has revealed that overweight people are less likely to be kidnapped.

I told my wife she ought to go on a diet.
She said she was already on two and another one would only add to her problem.

I told her a balanced diet was not a chocolate bar in each hand.

Morning Sermon: Jesus Walked on Water.

Evening Sermon: Looking for Jesus.

Snake 1: "Are we poisonous?"
Snake 2: "I don't know. Why?"
Snake 1: "I've just bitten my tongue."

"So, what's your hub password?"
"Go on, guess."
"Stop mucking about and just tell me what it is."
"That's unbelievable, you got it first time."

PUNISHING TIMES

Dominatrix: "In today's session we start with endless foreplay, and for a climax I beat you to within an inch of your life using a variety of implements, but only after you have used them to put up a couple of shelves for me."

The 'Flying Dutchman' pub in Camberwell is well known for its bondage workshops once a week. For newcomers it can last all week, until they learn the ropes.
Well, that's my excuse.

I invited a friend along, but she was already tied up.

I still had a spanking time though.

Interviewer: "And finally, Miss Jones, what would you say is your weakness, if you have one?"

Miss Jones: "Honesty, I think."

Interviewer: "Come now, I don't think that should be thought of as a weakness, really."

Miss Jones: "Perhaps, but frankly I don't give a damn what you think."

———————

One should never let old age get one down, especially as it's so hard getting up again.

————

I bent down to tie my shoelaces and thought, "This might be a good opportunity to re-polish the floor."

———————

Если вы не рискуете, вы никогда не пейте шампанское.

(Russian proverb) *

———————

I used to know a great joke about amnesia…

———————

I only ever told my grandfather one joke, and never once did he fail to laugh at it.

———————

I know what my first choice would be if the options were a painful death, buggery or Morris dancing.

Life today would be so much easier if you could auto-delete people too.

_____

And finally, to my best friend who wanted to be remembered in my will, "Hi, Jack."

_____

I joined the Society of Hermits and went to their AGM, but there was nobody there.

Their parties were rather singular too, reminiscent of a doctor's waiting room without the doctor.

_____

I am offended by those who claim to be offended, thereby giving them the right to trump my freedom of speech to offend them in the process of letting them know how I feel about their offensiveness.

_____

"I'm afraid I have bad and worse news, Mr Smith. The bad news is that I've just examined your wife and I'm afraid she has a cluster of sexually transmitted diseases."

"Good grief!" said Mr Smith. "If that's the bad news then what's the worse news?"

"You haven't."

_____

Sleeping pills and laxatives are a dangerous duo.

Lavatory humour is a funny old business.

———————

My windows are now so dirty I think the cleaner must have kicked his bucket.

———————

The pessimist thinks all women are bad.
The optimist hopes they are.

———————

A UCL study has revealed that 97.7% of statistics are wrong or simply made up.

———————

Once upon a time, there was a Prince who kissed a Princess, and look at me now.

———————

If time travel were possible, I'd be single again, somewhere else and only two hours late.

———————

Political correctness will be the death of humour.

———————

Of all my admirable qualities, I think the best is my modesty.

———————

Why is it easier to forgive one's enemies than one's friends?

———————

* (If you don't take risks, you never drink champagne.)

I'm not saying my girlfriend is a slut, but she does buy her knickers from Next, and wears them inside out and back to front.

———————

The USA and UK have agreed a new double taxation treaty. You send both of them all your credit card details and PIN numbers.

———————

It wasn't the job I was looking for, but at least it was paid employment.

———————

Political jokes cease to be funny once they are elected.

———————

It's easy to get into government if you are a lawyer, and easier still if you are one of their clients.

———————

First identify the problem, and then the scapegoat.

———————

My friend Mel writes very long letters without any punctuation at all which makes me wonder if she might be trying to outlive us all through asphyxiation.

———————

I don't understand why people keep arguing with me when I am right.

———————

His modesty was well deserved and recognised by all.

———————

My last thought every night is 'bugger them all'.

_____

If I were two-faced, I wouldn't be wearing this one.

_____

I only talk to myself when I need expert advice.

_____

Love thine enemies, in case your friends turn out to be a bunch of bastards.

_____

A friend in need will always be there when they need you again.

_____

My local health food shop is now selling organic dog biscuits. I didn't know there was such a breed.

_____

I taught my dog to beg, so now he buys his own food.

_____

I loved my teacher, but her bite was much worse than her bark.

_____

My dog is so stupid; yesterday I watched him chase his own tail, round and round for twenty minutes, until I fell over dizzy.

_____

On my birthday, my wife surprised me with a threesome, but I never got a turn.

Artist: "Tell me, please, what you think of my work."
Critic: "It's worthless."
Artist: "I know, but tell me anyway."

———————

I once had the perfect girlfriend, but when I accidentally bit her nipple, she farted and flew out of the window.

———————

My hedgehog Spike thinks he's funny. He wakes me up every morning by doing forward rolls on my chest.

The other day he had a hell of a scrap with the local fox, but in the end he managed to win on points.

His eyesight is now so poor, last week I caught him trying it on with the garden broom.

———————

A woman came home with her very first phone and went straight into the kitchen so that she could surprise her husband with a call from it.

"Darling, I've just bought myself a..."

Her husband whispered back, "Shush, I can't speak now, she's just come home and is in the kitchen."

———————

A woman and her lover are lying in bed enjoying a cigarette and afterglow, when her phone rings. After the brief conversation he asks who it was.

"Just my husband calling from the club to tell me how much he enjoyed beating the pants off you, as well."

I was most embarrassed when my first girlfriend asked me why I didn't have a hairy chest like her other boyfriends. So I told her, "Mummy shaves it for me when she does hers."

———————

I went on a blind date last night with a 30-year old who has six kids.

"No offence," I said, looking across the table. "But I thought it would just be the two of us."

———————

I met a fabulous girl at the dance last night but after I offered to run her home, not only did she beat me by 100 yards, when I got there the door was locked and the lights out.

———————

Weight Watchers Club members are advised to use both double doors at the rear of the church hall.

———————

My wife complained that the bedroom was untidy because she couldn't get everything into her drawers.

I told her it might help if she got back on her diet.

———————

War is God's way of teaching Americans a little about world geography.

———————

Why is it that Americans always mispronounce the countries they've invaded?

The world would have been so much safer if all its oil reserves had been in USA.

_____

In America, a pedestrian is a person who has just parked their car.

_____

America's biggest problem is obesity.

_____

America is the only nation in history that has gone from barbarism to decadence without the usual interval of civilisation.

_____

Many a true word is spoken in jest.

_____

God Bless America for giving us George Burns and Woody Allen.

_____

What would we do if the 'Don't Knows' won the election?

_____

Wife: "Sorry to disturb you at work, Darling, but the breakdown man has told me there's water in the carburettor."
Man: "That's most unlikely, it hasn't rained for days. Where are you?"
Wife: "I'm standing on the riverbank."

_____

We were so poor the mice brought their own cheese.

Wife: "Darling, the mechanic says we have a small problem with the handbrake, but the good news is that all the airbags have worked."

_____

Last week, I used the new Police On-line Crime Reporting service to report a theft from my shed.

This morning, I got an auto-reply text message from them telling me to come to the station as I was under arrest for wasting their time.

_____

Author: What's happened to the joke about the reluctant groom?

Publisher: We didn't like the look of the *vagina dentata* gag either, so we thought it better if we took it out, I'm afraid.

Author: I was afraid too, and quite disturbed by the state of the bride's gums.

_____

It's dangerous to drink and drive. If you brake sharply, you'll probably spill it.

_____

On some great and glorious day, the plain folks of this land will reach their heart's desire, and the White House will be adorned by a downright moron.

_____

I thought my wife had developed a speech impediment, but she was just pausing for breath.

COMMUNICATION BREAKDOWN 2

Judge: "Mrs Smith, can you outline for me the grounds for this divorce petition?"

Mrs S: "It's around four and a half acres, your Honour, with a pretty cottage hidden in the middle."

Judge: "Hmm, let me rephrase the question. What are the foundations of your case?"

Mrs S: "Don't know, your Honour, they're in the ground."

Judge: "Hmm, let me try a different approach. What are your relations like with your husband?"

Mrs S: "Well, your Honour, none of them like him."

Judge: "Oh dear, dear. Has your husband ever been unfaithful?"

Mrs S: "Well, he has never admitted it, but I know for sure he isn't the father of our kids."

Judge: "Now we are getting somewhere. So, moving on, has he ever beaten you?"

Mrs S: "Every day, your Honour, by about an hour, so that he can make his own breakfast."

Judge: "I'm afraid, I am at a loss to understand why you want this divorce?"

Mrs S: "It's not me, your Honour, it's him, because we never have a proper conversation together."

It's disrespectful to use your phone in church unless He called you.

_____

I never like disappointing people, so I always try to live up to their prejudices.

_____

Patient: "I'm really worried that when I touch my foot it hurts, and not just that, my knee, my shoulder, elbow, back, everything hurts when I touch it. What's wrong with me?"

Doctor: "It's nothing serious, you've just broken your finger."

_____

If God had intended us to fly, He wouldn't have created the TSA.

_____

In politics, one has come to expect more to mean worse.

_____

A fellow passenger spotted my Superman socks and expressed surprise that I was on a plane.

I told him I liked to take it easyJet now and again.

____

His companion sussed I might be a fraudster and asked me where I got them.

So, I told her they were a gift from my girlfriend, Lois.

Merry Christmas

I went on a blind date even though I'm not really a dog lover.

You know you are really drunk if you pass out and miss the floor.

My wife laid into me this morning for coming home drunk in the small hours and leaving my clothes in a heap on the bedroom floor.

Fortunately, she was so mad she didn't notice I hadn't taken them off.

Last week, I was too drunk to drive home, so I drove to another party.

If you were in my shoes, you'd be tired, drunk and looking for your shoes.

I'll always remember my father's last words to me.

"Was that my dialysis machine on eBay?"

I had an argument with the wife and now she won't talk to me.
I'll have to remember that one.

We were so poor we had our leftovers the day before.

It is popularly believed that Christopher Columbus discovered North America sometime after 1492. Despite there being a US national holiday celebrating this event, it is of course incorrect. Columbus only ever reached the Caribbean Islands and Central America.

The reality is that after hearing of a sighting of land to the west of Greenland by Icelander Bjarni Herjolfsson in 985 AD, Leif Eriksson, another Icelander, actually discovered North America and set foot there, most probably in the Canadian provinces of Newfoundland or New Brunswick.

Having done so, Eriksson returned home, telling his father, Erik the Red, who had fallen off his horse, hurt his back and had had to stay at home and missed the trip, that he had,

"Been there, done that, forget it."

I met a fabulous woman at a party last night. I hope to see her again, if I can remember where it was.

Ali: "Okay, so why is Christianity better than Islam?"
Ron: "Toasted bacon sandwiches."

It's a woman's prerogative to change her mind, if she has one.

A man's mind is always made up, until a woman changes it for him.

I got really drunk on my stag night but fortunately I sobered up in time for the divorce.

My mother liked the odd tipple or two. Sorry, I meant triple, which is where she lost count.

But she always insisted on everything being neat and tidy, including her gin and empties.

AFTER-SALES SERVICE

A husband returns home early and finding his wife's lover hiding in her wardrobe, he says, "Who are you, and what are you doing in there?"

The man replies, "Good afternoon, I'm the Customer Service Manager from IKEA, just checking your wife's wardrobe."

"Really, and why are you standing there dressed only in your socks?"

"I know it's a little indecent of me, but I couldn't find anything in here that suits me."

"OK, so what are you going to do about the missing knob?"

"Sorry, but I could have sworn I used it to get in here."

"I'm sure you did, but I was speaking figuratively about your future prospects."

I was heart-broken when my wife ran off with my best friend. I really miss him.

My wife hates the sight of me when I'm drunk, but then, when I'm sober I feel much the same about her.

In an almighty traffic jam in Central London, a police officer is passing from vehicle to vehicle talking to each driver.

"What's going on?" I asked.

"Terrorists have overrun Parliament and are holding the Members hostage. They've dowsed the place with petrol and threatening to burn it down unless an enormous ransom is paid immediately. So, we are asking people to chip in with whatever contributions they can afford, however small."

"Okay, Officer, I can let you have five litres."

When I was in my twenties my mother told me that if I still wanted her to iron my shirts, I needed to bring one home.

I only smoke at my age because it gives me something to hold on to.

When you start worrying about what awaits you at home, Happy Hour is there to cure it.

Why is it the best people to run the country are all cutting hair or driving cabs?

———————

I phoned an old girlfriend and asked if she was free on Monday night. "No," she said, she was now working full time and very busy, but happy to give me a discount.

Afterwards she said she regretted the offer, as the reunion had taken much longer than the last time.

———

Last night, I called another old girlfriend and she was really annoyed with me. She said that in her opinion forty-five wasn't old.

———

As I get older, I think it would be nice to see my old girlfriends again, but probably not all of them and certainly not in the same hall.

———————

I was so fed up with the neighbour's cat using my garden as a lavatory, I put some petrol in a saucer of milk for it.

After he lapped it all up, he shot around the garden ten times, ran up and down every tree twice and ended up motionless in the middle of the lawn on his back with his legs up in the air.

I thought, 'Crikey, I've killed it', but he was fine.

He'd just run out of petrol.

———————

That was some trick turning a spare rib into the Wrath of God.

A man never forgets his first time, unless he was drunk.

A woman never forgets her first time, but then they never forget anything, do they?

Two Irishmen walked past a pub because it was closed.

Once upon a time, you could have passed countless pubs on the Dock Road in Liverpool, but mostly you crawled into all of them.

Husbands' Rehabilitation Centre.

(Reykjavik bar sign)

Three weeks ago, my grandfather started walking five miles a day, and since we haven't had a single postcard from him, we have no idea where he is.

Long walks are especially good for people who annoy you.

I like long walks. I find the heavy breathing nostalgic.

When I read that lots of men find the size of Jennifer Lopez's bottom attractive, I thought I'd better lock my missus in the kitchen.

Women spend more time thinking about what men think about than the time that men actually think.

If they knew what men really thought about, they would probably hit the ceiling.

She 1: "I do like a man with a bit of a shady past."

She 2: "I'd rather have a man with a very nice present."

These days Amazon are into just about everything. Perhaps soon you'll be able to order your kids from them, and return them if they were unsuitable, defective or you just didn't like them.

A CD of a baby crying for two hours or a DVD of the same cartoon repeatedly would make great contraceptives.

I moved to the other end the country when I found the perfect pub. Now I can claim in all honesty that I was up at 'The Crack of Dawn' today.

Of all the newspapers I prefer the *Daily Mail*.
It's such an absorbing read and flushes quite well too.

I am sitting in the smallest room in my house with your review of my symphony in front of me.
In one short movement it will be behind me.

If it weren't for floating voters we'd all be sunk.

My friend Richard Penis was embarrassed by his name, so he changed it to Dick.

Oh dear, what can the matter be, my wife is locked in the lavatory, it's only Sunday not yet Saturday, so where will I go to weee?

The government's solution to a problem is always worse than the problem itself.

Beware of the greeting, 'I'm from the government and here to help.'

Actress: "I'm very versatile, you know, I even played a prostitute in Jack the Ripper."

Agent: "I assume you came to a sticky end?"

Actress: "Several times, actually."

If you cannot dazzle people with your brilliance, baffle them with bullshit.

Man: "The milkman was in the pub last night, drunk and bragging that he had slept with every woman in the street, except one of course."

Wife: "I'll bet it's that snotty cow at no.19."

_____

My wife left me after I commented on the neglected housework. Coincidentally, the milkman, the gardener and the window cleaner never returned either.

_____

I've been driving now for 50 years and never been involved in an accident. Mind you, I've seen plenty in my rear-view mirror.

_____

Having children on the back seats of cars can be the cause of accidents, and vice versa.

_____

Where there's a will, I want to be in it.

_____

The last thing I want to do is hurt you, but it is still on my list.

_____

I'm not surprised the Titanic sank, with all that seawater in its swimming pool.

_____

War does not determine who is right, only who is left.

_____

If I agreed with you, we'd both be wrong.

———————

They begin the news with "Good Evening," and then proceed to tell you why it isn't.

———————

To steal ideas from one person is plagiarism.
To steal from many is research.

———————

Buses stop at bus stations, and trains stop at train stations. My desk is a work station.

———————

I could tell the burglars were gay by the way they had rearranged my wardrobe.

———————

Myth 8: Religion and politics are different.

———————

Women will never be equal to men, until they can strut down the street with a bald head and a beer belly and think they are still sexy.

———————

Behind every successful man is a woman.
Behind every unsuccessful man there are usually one or two more.

———————

You do not need a parachute to skydive unless you plan to do it twice.

Money can't buy happiness, but it does make your misery more comfortable.

_____

I thought I was indecisive but now I'm not so sure.

_____

My dog loves children, especially their bones.

_____

Wife: "Honey, I'm home. Notice anything different?"
Him: "You've had your hair done."
Wife: "No."
Him: "You've got a new outfit?"
Wife: "No."
Him: "New shoes?"
Wife: "No."
Him: "Okay, I give up."
Wife: "I'm wearing a gas-mask."

_____

There's quite a difference between cuddling and pinning someone down so they can't get away.

_____

You're never too old to learn something stupid.

_____

To be sure of hitting the target, shoot first and call whatever you hit the target.

_____

Nostalgia really isn't what it used to be.

_____

Change is inevitable, except from a vending machine.

———————

Going to church doesn't make you a good person any more than standing in a garage makes you a mechanic.

———————

Where there's a will, there are usually relatives.

———————

I spilt some stain remover on my shirt and don't know what to use to get it out.

———————

My wife is always having accidents in the kitchen, but still expects me to eat them.

———————

I told my wife that 90% of accidents happen in the home and that was the last I saw of her.

———————

I don't trust the bank with my money. They wanted a password eight characters long, and when I chose 'Snow White and the Seven Dwarfs' they said that was too many.

———————

Apparently, half of British men have no idea how to turn on a washing machine. I find that flowers or chocolates do the trick.

———————

We were so poor Christmas only came once a year.

The way into a woman's bed is to warm her up with a few jokes, but save your best for the side-splitting finale when you drop your trousers.

———————

Wife: "Doctor, I've got this dreadful pain in the neck and I can't get rid of it. First, it's on one side then the other, and it rarely goes away."
Doctor: "OK, so where is it now?"
Wife: "In his shed."

———————

I think all politicians should be restricted to two terms with the second one in prison.

———————

Wife: "Great news, I've won the lottery, so pack your bags."
Him: "Where are we going?"
Wife: "I've booked a luxury cruise around the world, while you find your own place."

———————

I thought I was Casanova reincarnated when my wife ripped me to shreds during orgasms.
Then I discovered she was faking them.

———————

The French are forever whinging about English being the international language of choice. They just need to accept it's a *fait accompli.*

———————

Borrow money from pessimists; they'll never expect it back.

There's no hope for humanity when half the people in the world are still below average intelligence.

———————

99% of lawyers give the rest a bad name.

———————

A conscience is what hurts when the rest of you feels good.

———————

I nearly had a psychic girlfriend, but she dumped me just before we met.

———————

If everything is going well, you have obviously overlooked something, or miscounted the idiots.

———————

If time travel were ever possible, someone should have come back to eliminate Trump's barber.

———————

My wife came home from the beauty salon after one of those mud pack treatments and looked fantastic for two days, until it all fell off.

———————

No man or woman is worth the loss of a good night's sleep.

———————

Two nihilists fell in love when they saw they had nothing in common.

They say marriage is a fine institution, but you need to be committed to live in one.

_____

Now I've joined AA, I can drink under a false name.

_____

When I was knocked over by the mobile library and lay groaning in the road, the driver rushed over and told me to be quiet.

_____

Young man: "Do you think I'm vain?"
Young lady: "Not at all; why do you ask?"
Young man: "Good looking guys like me often are."

_____

Politician: "It took me five years to finish my book."
Voter: "Was it long, or are you just a slow reader?"

_____

Man: "Haven't I seen you somewhere before?"
Woman: "Yes, that was when I stopped going there."

_____

I used to know another joke about amnesia, but it's probably the same one.

_____

Democracy and mob rule are close companions.

_____

Never put both feet in your mouth at the same time, or you won't have a leg to stand on.

KFC claim that their new genetically modified four legged chickens are tastier, but this is unverified as no one has managed to catch one yet.

_____

Woman 1: "Men are all the same; they just have different faces so that you can tell them apart."

Woman 2: "I don't see the point, since I always keep my eyes closed anyway."

_____

Jack: "I don't think much of your tailor. That suit is a terrible fit, and why is it so crumpled?"

Tony: "I know, but it was a surprise birthday present that the wife had stuffed under the bed."

_____

Men's genitalia are proof that God is a woman, and with a wicked sense of humour.

_____

I inherited my misogyny from my dear mother.

_____

Whenever the needs arise to write to my MP, I like to remind him of our relationship by signing off with,

"You remain my obedient servant..."

_____

His paranoia got him in the end.

_____

MEN ARE JUST HAPPIER

Your last name stays put.
The garage is all yours.
Wedding plans take care of themselves.
Chocolate is just another snack.
You can never be pregnant.
You can wear a T-shirt to a water park.
You can wear no shirt to a water park.
Car mechanics tell you the truth.
The world is your urinal.
Petrol station toilets are never too 'yucky.'
You know which way to turn a nut on a bolt.
Same work, more pay.
Wrinkles add character.
Wedding dress £2,000, suit rental £100.
People never stare at your chest when talking to you.
New shoes don't cut, blister, or mangle your feet.
One mood all the time.
Phone calls never take more than a minute.
You know stuff about tanks.
A holiday only requires one suitcase.
You can open all your own jars.
If she forgets to invite you, she can still be your friend.
Your underwear is £8.95 for a three-pack.
Three pairs of shoes are more than enough.
You never have strap problems in public.
You are unable to see wrinkles in your clothes.
Everything on your face stays its original colour.
The same hairstyle lasts for decades.
You only need to shave your face and neck.
You can do your own nails with a penknife.
A moustache is your choice.
You can wear shorts no matter how your legs look.
You can play with toys all your life.

Clairvoyant: "I see a long slow agonising death for your husband."
Mrs Smith: "Oh dear, but do I get away with it?"

———————

I went shopping with my wife yesterday. She tried on ten red dresses before choosing the red one.

———————

My girlfriend accused me of being childish, and it was she who wouldn't return my Xbox.

———————

Getting old is no fun. Today, I had to fasten my wife's bra for her. It only seems like yesterday that she had to undo it for me.

———————

All some parents ask of their children is a bit of credit for the sacrifices they have made.

I'd rather have a full cash refund.

———————

Tony: "Where did you get all those jokes?"
Jack: "They were in a book I wrote."

———————

I just read that Brighton is now within striking distance of London, but that must be true of all union staffed stations.

———————

Myth 9: Pedestrianisation of London's Oxford Street will 'improve the shopping experience'.

Lady: "Are there any good cheap hotels in this area that you can recommend?"

Guide: "A lady friend tells me the best one is opposite the station where they only charge £10 an hour."

My wife thinks housework should be just one sweeping glance of the room.

It's nice to feel wanted, as long as it's not by the authorities.

Once upon a time, complimenting a woman on her good-looking legs would not have been regarded as sexual harassment.

Although, asking her if they are just as nice all the way up to her bottom might have been going just a little bit too far.

Jack: "Why do we expect to marry a virgin? I mean, I slept with my wife before we married. What about you?"

Ron: "I don't know. What was her maiden name?

If ignorance were bliss he would have been the happiest boy in school.

The school Mountaineering Club used to meet once a week on the chapel roof, where we felt closer to God.

INEVITABLE

A man and his wife go to the doctor for a consultation about his illness. As they leave, the doctor calls the wife back in alone and says,

"I'm afraid your husband has a very serious stress-related illness, and I didn't want to aggravate his mental state by telling him about his fragile condition and the care that he needs to take if he wants to survive. From now on, he needs utmost rest, and a regular diet of healthy nutritious meals, foods that he likes and enjoys. Avoid forcing him to eat foods that he doesn't like even though they might be good for him. You should also make sure that he cuts down on his drinking, but if he fancies a tipple or two with his evening meal to keep him happy and invigorated, the choice should be limited to fine wines, in moderate quantities. He should be encouraged to rest as much as he can, and I suggest you discourage him from exerting himself doing household repairs and any other routine daily chores about the house. If you keep to this regime for the next twelve months, there is an excellent chance that he will recover from his current physical condition and depressed mental state and pull through. But he will need you as a constant companion to nurse him along."

Outside the surgery, the man asks his wife what the doctor had said to her.

She replied, "You're going to die."

_____

I think my hedgehog Spike has become romantically attached to my new beard.

One morning, little Johnny catches his parents making love.

"Daddy, what are you doing to Mummy?" he asks.

"We are making a baby sister for you," says his father.

Johnny replies, "Well, tell Mummy to turn over. I'd rather have a puppy."

———————

Life is full of opportunities to keep your mouth shut.

———————

I accidentally swallowed my Scrabble tiles, and so my next trip to the lavatory could spell disaster.

———————

"I'm not schizophrenic, and neither am I," he said.

———————

Police Officer: "Where are you going at this time of night, and driving so slowly?"

Elderly driver: "I am on my way to a lecture about alcohol abuse and the effects it has on the human body, as well as smoking and staying out late."

Police Officer: "Oh really, and just who is giving such a lecture at this time of night?"

Elderly driver: "My wife."

———————

My genius has nothing to declare.

During my survey on shower gel preferences, 89 out of 92 women responded with,

"How the hell did you get in here?"

Dear Mel

In my haste, or perhaps it was someone else, I left your party with a lovely pair of lace scanties stuffed into my jacket pocket. I must admit, I find them enormously exciting and if they are yours, I would love to return them to you as soon as I find my cycle clips.

If they are not yours, perhaps you can set aside any female rivalries and circulate my discovery to your lady guests, inviting them to attend a private fitting session at my place this coming Saturday at 2pm.

In view of my urgency, RSVPs may be dispensed with, but fully attired claimants should form an orderly queue outside no.11 and are requested to maintain a level of decorum.

However, I do hope that we can dispense with all of that, and perhaps with the scanties too, and that together we can explore any other deficiencies in your wardrobe.

Txxx

Lies travel a damn sight faster than the truth.

We were so poor even my tortoise took in lodgers.

A woman goes to see her psychiatrist.

She: "Can you cure my nymphomania?"
He: "I can, but it will be expensive."
She: "How much is expensive?"
He: "My standard rate is £200 an hour."
She: "How much for a whole night?"

Man: "Can I help you?"
Caller: "I've come to tune your piano."
Man: "But I didn't request a tuner."
Caller: "No, it was your neighbours."

A wife asks her husband if he would ever marry again if she died.

He: "No, dear, I would miss you so much, and couldn't bear the thought of taking up with anyone else."

She: "But that's silly. You would have this large house all to yourself, that you'd have to clean, and you'd have to do all your own cooking, and just for one person. And my new car would just be sitting in the garage, unused. And, surely, you'd like to see someone using my new set of golf clubs?"

He: "No, she's left-handed."

Like nappies, politicians need changing at regular intervals and for similar reasons.

My girlfriend asked me for an example of a *double entendre*, so I gave her one.

———————

He: "Do you know the difference between conversation and sex?"
She: "No."
He: "Well, lie down, I'd like to talk to you."

———————

BBC BROKEN NEWS: ROBIN HOOD'S REMAINS DISCOVERED

Due to the absence of any remains, it has long been assumed that Robin Hood was a mythical figure dating from the 12th Century. The legend tells of his dying request to be buried wherever his final arrow fell, and for centuries the search was focused within the historical confines of Sherwood Forest, most of which has succumbed to centuries of building development.

Yesterday, what are now thought to be his indisputable remains were discovered by a Liverpool auctioneer cataloguing an upcoming sale, when he found a skeleton, green fabric remnants and an arrow stuffed inside an 11th Century wardrobe.

———————

I love that whooshing sound that deadlines make as they fly by.

———————

I often confuse Americans and Canadians, mostly with long English words or world news.

Bookseller: "Can I help you, sir?"
Browser: "I'm looking for a book by Shakespeare."
Bookseller: "Of course, which one would that be?"
Browser: "William, I expect."

Dear Mel,

Thank you for this year's Christmas party invitation generously extended to partners and friends.

My supporting cast and fan club are all extremely excited and would like to know if they can reserve a space outside to park their coach.

I will arrive in advance and look forward to assisting you with any last-minute adjustments to your wardrobe.

Txxx

I dislike people who assume you're rich just because you went to public school, speak properly, have excellent taste, wealthy friends and a butler.

The fool only questions others and never himself.

A suicide bomber asked his doctor for a sick note.

After my morning ablutions, I weighed in 10 pounds lighter than yesterday, which only confirms what a lot of people have been saying about me.

NO COMEBACK

The senior members of the Board of Directors of the company were called into the Chairman's office one by one until only Jack, the junior member, was left sitting outside.

Finally, when he was summoned in, he found the chairman and the other directors seated around a table.

As soon as he sat down the chairman turned to Jack, looked him squarely in the eye, and with a stern voice, asked,

"Have you ever had sex with my secretary?"

"No", he ejaculated.

"Are you absolutely sure?" asked the Chairman.

"Honestly, I've never been close enough to even touch her!"

"You'd swear to that?"

"Yes, I swear I've never had sex with Mrs. Crabtree anytime, anywhere."

"Excellent, you can fire her."

————————

I don't mind arguing with idiots providing none of them agree with me.

Paddy is in court yet again for punching his wife.

Judge: "Tell me, Mr Molloy, why do you keep beating her?"
Paddy: "I think it's my weight advantage, longer reach and superior footwork."

———————

(This text has been intercepted by the CIA, FBI, and NSA)

———————

A Scouser goes to the doctor and says, "I've become a serious kleptomaniac. What can I take for it?"

The doctor writes out a prescription and says, "Take three of these tablets, three times a day for the next three weeks, and when they don't work, I could do with a new computer."

———————

To speed up wheel changes, Scuderia Ferrari hired their pit crew from Liverpool. It was a great idea, except they also managed to give the car a tune-up and respray and sell it to Mercedes.

———————

My friend Mel is on her phone, non-stop. I tried sending her a text all day yesterday explaining the concept of punctuation and breathing, but that was engaged too.

PRIVATE MATTERS

Scene: Doctors Waiting Room, full of patients.

Elderly patient: "I don't have an appointment, but I need to see a Doctor today, please?"

Young receptionist: "Only if it's an emergency or very serious; we are fully booked."

Elderly patient: "It is serious and possibly an emergency."

Young receptionist loudly: "What exactly is the problem?"

Elderly patient, even louder: "I have this enormous swelling on my penis that wasn't there yesterday, but I woke up this morning with it really throbbing. It might just be a massive erection, but I think it should be checked out. Do you need to see it?"

Young receptionist blushing: "Doctor will see you now."

———————

Mother used to say, "an apple a day keeps the doctor away".
Today, I find a bacon sandwich just as effective.

———————

I've been happily married for ten years, which isn't bad out of twenty-five.

———————

This book is unsuitable for anyone who cannot read.

A NORTHERN TAIL

A car breaks down in a remote part of Iceland. The man gets out, lifts the bonnet and scratching his head stares at the engine. Just then a voice behind him says, "It's the carburettor." When he turns around he is startled to see a horse looking over his shoulder, and in panic he runs off.

Eventually he comes to a farmhouse, where he recounts to the farmer the details of the incident. The farmer frowns and asks the colour of the horse, to which the man replies that it was dappled brown.

The farmer says, "You were right to ignore him; that one doesn't know anything about engines."

————————

"I have looked at the sea through my tears."

————————

A little girl goes shopping with her daddy, and after visiting the cake shop, they go to the barber's where she sits down next to him while he has a haircut.

The barber warns her, "Be careful, little girl, you're going to get hair on your muffin."

She replies, "I know, and I'm going to grow some tits, too".

————————

Patient: "I think I have a touch of hypochondria."
Doctor: "No problem, try these placebos."
Patient: "Thanks, and see you again tomorrow."

FACEBOOK FOR SENIORS

I am trying to make new friends by following the same principles and procedures used by Facebook users, but without a phone or the Internet.

So, every day I walk down the street and tell my neighbours, friends, casual acquaintances and passers-by what I have eaten, how I feel now, what I did yesterday, what I will do later and with whom. I give pictures of my family, my dog, me gardening, taking things apart in the garage, putting things back together again, driving around town, standing in front of assorted buildings, having lunch, and generally doing all sorts of everyday things that I find not particularly interesting or even boring. I also encourage everybody I meet to swap stories, anecdotes, and pictures etc. I listen to them intently, give them the 'thumbs-up' as often as I can, and I tell them all that I like them.

It's great, it works, and after one week I already have a string of followers – a psychiatrist, two policemen, three nurses, four store security guards, five beggars and a bunch of giggling children.

Do stop me if you see me in the street.

———————

Outside the station last night, I saw this woman with the longest legs and most glorious chest I had ever come across. Call me naïve, but I had to stop and ask her what she was selling and how much?

If you know who she is, please let me know as my case comes up next week.

BBC BROKEN NEWS: NW CRIME REPORT

Police in Liverpool last night announced the discovery of an arms cache of 200 semi-automatic pistols with 25,000 rounds of ammunition, 2 tons of heroin, £5 million in forged UK banknotes and 25 Ukrainian prostitutes, all in a semi-detached house behind Toxteth Public Library.

A local resident said, "We're all really surprised; we never knew it was a library."

A third of Britons are conceived in an IKEA bed, which is surprising as their showrooms are very brightly lit.

"I'm sorry but I fell asleep while you were talking."

You know winter is coming when M&S in Liverpool reopen their knicker department.

GOLF CLUB

Members are asked to refrain from picking up lost balls until they have stopped rolling.

The club captain asked what my handicap was, so I told him, I can't play and I don't have the balls for it.

My dating agency matched me up with my ex-wife.

GAME, SET and MATCH

At the Tennis Club, the locker room is full of men in various stages of undress. A mobile phone goes off in a half open locker, and a naked man rushes out of the showers and snatching up the phone, says:

"Hi, Darling… Yes, I'm still at the club… No, he beat me in the first round… Yes, then a drink with the boys… Well, if you really need the matching handbag… No, 2000 is okay… I love you too, Darling… The new car?... Well, if you think it's worth 90,000 and you really want it, it should be fully loaded… Okay, then order it… Really, the penthouse is back on the market… A million?... Try offering 900, and if pushed go to 950, but no more, not just yet… Okay, I love you too, Sweetie… Speak later… No, I can't, she's arranged a night at the opera for our anniversary… But I am okay tomorrow night… Yes, yes, those real skimpy see-through ones would be great… Bye, bye, x x x."

He turns around to face a room full of speechless men all gaping at him, and putting the phone back, says,

"That'll teach the bastard."

_____

The best way to make a life of crime pay is to become a lawyer.

_____

One should hold one's convictions lightly.

_____

Am I a figment of my own imagination?

I THINK THEREFORE I DRINK.

Men who judge women on their looks are so sexist and shallow. I like to explore those other female attributes, like cooking and cleaning.

———————

Police Officer: "Dr Schrödinger, did you know you have a dead cat on the back seat of your car?"

Schrödinger: "Well, I do now."

———

Police Officer: "Dr Heisenberg, can you tell me how fast you were going when the other car hit you?"

Heisenberg: "Get in and I'll try to explain…"

———————

Drinker 1: "I lost my job due to illness and fatigue."
Drinker 2: "What happened?"
Drinker 1: "My boss was sick and tired of me."

———————

Dr A: "Hello, what can I do for you today?"
Jack: "I need something for a nagging pain."
Dr A: "Of course, where is it exactly?"
Jack: "Somewhere in the shopping centre."

———————

My wife spent ages in the bathroom getting dressed to go out when finally, the door swung open and she said, "Do I look big in this?"

I said, "Yes darling, but to be fair, it is a very small room."

———————

A true test of faith is whether you can afford to put your last twenty on the collection plate.

———

If money is the root of all evil why do they collect it in church and use it for renovations?

———

Until 1945 the best all-terrain vehicle was the Sherman tank. Since then it's been the rental car.

———

I called the dating agency and they told me it was the Ides of March.

———

I thought my new girlfriend might be the one for me, but after looking through her smalls' drawer and finding a nurse's uniform, a maid's outfit, and a police uniform, I decided if she can't hold down a job, she's not for me.

———

I got home the other night and couldn't find the wife anywhere.
Turns out she had found a nicer place, changed her name and forgot to tell me.

———

Political Correctness is a new form of censorship that if left unchallenged will silence you, overwrite your opinions and ultimately rewrite history.

———

Reality is the first symptom of alcohol deficiency.

A disabled man is taken to Lourdes hoping for a miracle cure. His carer pushed his wheelchair into the waters and left him there for the miracle to happen. After only ten minutes, the man emerged unaided from the waters with a new set of tyres.

When I was small, my father had really high ambitions for me and apprenticed me to a local chimney sweep.

I didn't like my first beard, so I grew another one.

I didn't like that one either but then it started to grow on me.

W.I. CALENDAR

Ladies, the Spring Rummage Sale is your chance to get rid of all those things you no longer use or need at home. Husbands also welcome.

I'm reading a book on gravity but it's very heavy going.

The other book is about anti-gravity which I haven't been able to put down.

My Superman socks were a big disappointment. Not only could I not fly, but after three weeks they needed washing.

"Doctor, I've got ten kids and all the contraceptives you've ever prescribed just haven't worked."

"Well, maybe you should try this new one?"

"It's massive; I can't swallow that?"

"You don't. You just hold it between your knees."

An optical illusion just looks like one.

TUNNEL VISION

The gynaecologist decided he wanted a career change and enrolled on a car mechanic's course.

In his final practical exam, he got an incredible 150%. When he queried how this was possible, the examiner explained,

"You got 50% for the perfect strip-down of the engine, and you got another 50% for a perfect repair and reassembly."

"Yes, but what about the other 50%?"

"Well, you completed both sections through the exhaust pipe."

Inspector: "I think the circumstantial evidence is now overwhelming, and at last we have identified the serial killer. You're under arrest, Miss Marple."

PERFORMANCE REVIEW

"I think we need to meet and discuss my role in your company."

"Good idea, but I'm tied up with someone else right now, but should be free in thirty minutes or so."

"Excellent, what time and where?"

"Let's say forty minutes, my bedroom."

———————

St Peter at the Pearly Gates: "Sorry, Jesus, we don't do nepotism here, and we don't need any conjurers just now."

———————

If you are not part of the solution, you may have been identified as the problem.

———————

I have reached the age when my disappointments far outnumber any remaining ambitions.

———————

He was a man held hostage by his own family.

———————

No man has ever been shot while doing the dishes.

———————

The Liverpool Registry Office and the Maternity Hospital are conveniently located on the same street only 19.52 seconds apart.

PRIORITIES

A man wakes up in hospital and says to the doctor, "Where am I, what happened?"

The doctor replies, "You were in a very bad traffic accident, badly mutilated, and you have been in a coma for the past six months. In the meantime, with your insurance award we have reconstructed your face from your old photographs, pieced together your shattered hands, carried out extensive skin grafts and replaced a few vital organs. You are almost as good as new..."

The man interrupts, "But I can't feel my groin..."

The doctor, "Ah yes, that is one area we were reluctant to address. In the crash you lost your penis, and since we didn't have any photos to work from, and your wife's memory of it was rather vague, we decided to leave it until you could advise us further. You don't need to worry though, because you still have more than double the money we need to reconstruct it, so no problem."

The man says, "Hell, let's spend it all!"

The doctor replies, "Well, before you get carried away, this is a sensitive area, and we advise caution. We recommend that patients consult their partners before deciding how far to go with a rebuild, so, when she visits you later you need to come to a mutual decision."

The next day, the doctor asks how the talk went, to which the man replies,

"We've decided to have a new kitchen."

A synonym is useful when you can't spell the other word.

"Knock, knock."
"Who's there?"
"The doorbell repair man."

Surprise sex is a nice thing to wake up to, unless you're in prison.

Age is a high price to pay for experience.

"Say when," the man says as he pours her a cocktail.
"Okay", she says, "right after this drink."

Thanks to political correctness, I have had to change my dog's name from Nigger to Boy.

Two nuns were riding their tandem through the cobbled backstreets of Rome.

Nun1: "I've never come this way before."
Nun 2: "Yes, it's is so much quicker and longer too."

My one regret in life is that I am not someone else.

Today, so many lies we hear are true, and vice versa.

It's good to start the day by getting out of bed, even if it spoils the rest of the day.

———————

Sometimes, I like to live life dangerously and disagree with the wife.

———————

St Peter at the Pearly Gates: "Who are you lot and what do you want?"

Forty football fans in unison: "We are all loyal Liverpool supporters, we have season tickets and travel to every away game. And on our way home our coach crashed and we all died."

St Peter: "Wait here while I check with the boss if that is sufficient to let you in." And off he goes to relay the story to God.

God: "You can't trust Scousers! You'd better check they are all dead."

So, off he shuffles and returns after a couple of minutes, saying, "It's alright, they've gone."

God: "All of them?"

St Peter: "Yes, and the gates too."

———————

My wife claims to be the fount of all knowledge which at times is a blessing, but all too often a curse.

TIME TRAVEL AND TENSES

After recovering from a long illness and a subsequent two years of unemployment, my friend Jack was delighted when, on 7th December 2017, he received an email dated the previous day inviting him to an interview for the post of shop manager at the local Oxfam shop. The trouble was that the date of the interview was 21st September 2017.

In desperation Jack asked me if I thought there might be a way of travelling back in time so that he could attend the interview, but then he realised that since he did not currently have the job, he must have failed the interview. Either that, or he was unable to find the means of time-travel in time for the interview and lost the job because he failed to attend. But then his worries deepened when he realised that if he did manage to attend the interview and got the job, what would have happened on 6th December when it was time for the email to be sent to him.

After all, he realised, if he attended the interview in September and was appointed to the position, then there would no longer be a vacancy, and the email advertising it wouldn't be sent out. In which case, he wouldn't be able to respond to it.

And then, Jack wondered if time travel were possible, would he be better off going forward in time to collect all his future unemployment benefits to pay for his forthcoming holiday, if that had proven to have been worthwhile going on, in the future.

But then he realised that by going forward in time, he would be bypassing his imminent experiences, and would only retain his memories of events that he had not actually experienced, unless he could go back once again to enjoy them as they occurred. But would he be able to transport with him artefacts of the future to an earlier time before which they had begun to exist.

And what if going forward in time took him beyond an event or series of events that removed vital experiences that were crucial to his future existence, and without his accumulated knowledge of those events of which he would have been unaware. And how would he know any of this, if it was real or not, or just a memory of something that might have never happened, or would never have happened in the past, or the future.

In the end, Jack decided to wait and see what didn't happen.

———————

My Doctor prescribed half a Viagra tablet every night. I said, "Why do I need that? I'm not married." He said, "I know, but it will stop you rolling out of bed."

———————

The only thing standing between me and greatness is me.

———————

We were so poor the first one up got to wear the shoes.

A wife says to her husband, "Can you go to the shop and buy a carton of milk, and if they have any avocados get six."

When he returns with the milk, his wife asks, "Why did you buy six cartons of milk?"

He replied, "They had avocados."

A CONVERSATION UPSTAIRS

God: "I'm giving up on those folk downstairs, Son. Where did they dream up the Devil?"

Jesus: "It beats the hell out of me."

God: "And, did we ever find out what Noah did with the dinosaurs? I mean, how could anyone miss something that size?"

Jesus: "They never look properly. I did all those tricks two thousand years ago, and they still haven't figured any of them out."

God: "By the way, how did you do the one with the loaves and fishes?"

Jesus: "It was easy; I switched the fish with a couple of dinosaurs."

Jack: "I woke up grumpy this morning."
Tony: "I don't bother. I let her sleep in."

I got home from the pub after a heavy night with the boys and found the wife had not only changed the locks, she'd also changed the house, and the street.

Apparently, multitasking does not include headaches and sex.

My dictionary defines a housekeeper as a woman with a good lawyer.

Jack: "Am I the first man to make love to you?"
Trish: "You could be, your face is very familiar."

A man walks into a crowded bar in downtown Miami armed with a pair of Magnums and yells,
"I want to know which of you jerks has been sleeping with my wife?"
A voice from the back of the bar calls out,
"Hey, Buster, you need to come back with more ammo."

I'd rather read a software licence agreement than argue with a woman.

I went to the doctor and asked her if she could give me something for my erectile dysfunction.

She said, "Take three of these tablets, three times a day for the next three days, and if they work, come back and we can give each other a thorough examination."

A QUESTION

Dear Sir,

Some years ago, I married a widow who has an 18-year old daughter. Following several visits, my widowed father fell in love with my step-daughter, after which he took her on holiday and secretly married her. Because of that marriage, my step-daughter also became my step-mother, my father became my son-in-law, and my wife became my father's mother-in-law. A year later, my father's wife gave birth to a son, being my wife's grandson and my half-brother, and therefore my wife's brother-in-law, who because I am her husband is also my grandson. As a result, I am simultaneously my wife's grandson and my half-brother's grandfather, thus making my father his own son's father and great-grandfather. A short time after this birth, my wife also gave birth to a son, who is clearly my father's and step-mother's grandson. However, at the same time, my son is also my step-daughter's half-brother which makes him my father's and step-mother's brother-in-law, and in turn makes my son my own uncle. At the same time, through my step-mother, my wife has become a great-grandmother to her own son, and by my marriage to her, I have also become my son's great-grandfather, making him my father's great-great-grandson as well as grandson.

Can you advise me of any eligibility for family benefits, and who can claim what and for whom?

Yours very faithfully,

Mohammed Ali al-Jehadi

AN ANSWER

Dear Mr al-Jehadi

It certainly is a complex family question. However, the answer is very simple.

As newcomers to the UK, all your relatives will qualify for dependants' benefits for each of their relationships with you and with each other.

Although the number of individuals in your family is relatively small, it cannot be overlooked that the complexity of the multiple relationships technically expands that number to a total of twenty, and probably many more.

As soon as you arrive, you will need to arrange permanent accommodation for all your family with the local housing authority, so that you can receive your full entitlements.

In view of your extensive needs, I would recommend London as your port of entry, where any of the local councils who are legally obligated to accommodate all family members together in one dwelling, will have little difficulty in requisitioning a small hotel for you.
If you can demonstrate a prior high standard of living in your country of origin, you may be able to claim five-star accommodation with full-time room service thrown in.

Undoubtedly, you will rightly think you have hit the jackpot, but a word of caution. All your income, whatever its source and earned or not, must be fully and correctly declared to the tax authorities.

And, any assessed taxes must be fully and promptly paid. However, this should not have any detrimental effect on your living standards or aspirations, as in the event of any insufficiencies in your net income, you and your dependants will be entitled to claim both supplementary benefits and emergency hardship payments, to allow you to maintain your adopted life-style at the same level as any other UK resident living in similar accommodation.

Free or subsidised travel passes are also available to anyone dependent on income support, but if you plan to travel around the country by train to meet up with your friends, I would advise you to take your own folding chair with you, so that you do not have to sit on the floor.

If you have any further questions, please write directly to my secretary and expert in these matters, Mohammed al-Murakibi.

Welcome to the UK.

Jeremy

Scene: Globe Theatre, London, dress rehearsal.

Patrick Stewart: "A horse, a horse, my kingdom for a horse, else the day is lost to our enemy the Borg."

Director: "Patrick, stop there, please. We're doing Richard III, not Star Trek…"

Patrick Stewart: "I know, but Shakespeare is boring and there aren't any spaceships in it."

When I followed my friend Mel's advice to go on an exotic Greek holiday filled with wine, women and song, it turned out to be a disappointing waste of time. I felt like a fish out of water on Lesbos.

"Do Not Touch" must be a scary message in braille.

Procrastination is not recommended for people with short memories.

I thought I was hearing voices in my head, and then I realised I still had my headphones on.

I tell people I have an unbelievable sex life, and they never believe it.

It was the presents and chocolate that converted my children to Christianity.

Ring ring… ring ring…

"Hello, I understand you were recently involved in a traffic accident?"

"That's correct, but unfortunately all occupants of both cars including myself were killed, and so I am only taking calls now until my battery dies on me too."

"I'm sorry to hear that; I'll let you rest in peace."

LONDON LATEST
CITY CHOKED
TO STANDSTILL
AS CYCLISTS
HIJACK ROADS

Current cosmology theory is that the Big Bang at the centre of the universe was sparked by a collision of two enormous clusters of egotists and narcissists.

When my psychiatrist told me I was clinically insane, I told him I wanted a second opinion.
He said I was stupid too.

Myth 10: One-way streets and banned turns, extending travel distances and journey times onto constricted routes made narrower by cycle and bus lanes, all with excessively low speed limits and other obstacles help reduce traffic congestion and pollution.

One day I arrived home from school, and found my father had put the wheels back on it and driven off.

To be born a gentleman is a privilege, but to die one is an honour.

At 6 o'clock this morning, I was rudely awakened by the postman rattling the letterbox. When I opened the door, he demanded an instantly payable 20p excess charge for a letter with insufficient postage on it.

Fortunately, I wear my money belt under my pyjamas.

One thing in life that is worse than death is an evening with an insurance salesman.

BRIEF ENCOUNTERS

Dear Alice

Thank you for your splendid company at the charity dinner this week. It was a pleasure meeting you, and your rather youthful mum.

I am sure we have met several times previously in or around Kings Cross Station, either you or your double with the same persistent mischievousness.

And thank you for mistaking my age; perhaps you too should try Specsavers.

Txxx

———

Hello Tony,

What a pleasant surprise having you pop up in my inbox this morning.

It was an enormous pleasure to meet you again, but I don't know what I was thinking of, playing the 'age-game' when under the influence of drink, half way under the table, and in my own time too.

I hope you will be lurking in town as well next week, and if so, my new pitch is opposite Platforms 6 and 7.

Axxxx

———

There is always one more idiot than you expected.

I love the gold pocket watch that my grandfather sold to me on his deathbed.

_____

Sex without love is a meaningless experience, but as far as meaningless experiences go, it's pretty good.

_____

I don't want immortality through my achievements. I want it by not dying.

_____

You could live to be a hundred if you gave up all the things that make you want to live to be a hundred.

_____

I think my wife likes me more drunk when she is too.

_____

If only God would give me a clear sign, like making a large deposit in my name at a Swiss Bank.

_____

In passing sentence, the Judge said to the man,
"You almost committed the proverbial perfect crime that would have avoided detection. So, why did you leave your wife's bare backside sticking out of the front garden lawn?"
The man replied,
"I couldn't dig the hole any deeper and thought maybe no one would notice if I used it to park my bike."

_____

To err is human, hence the rubber on the end of your pencil.

If it turns out there is a God, I think the worst you could say about him is that he's an underachiever.

_____

It's not that I'm afraid of dying, I just don't want to be there when it happens.

_____

I am still in hospital after the traffic accident with a steamroller. I am fine, but the doctor has told me it will be a very long recovery.

_____

Women marry men with the hope they will change. Men marry women hoping they won't.

That's the power of optimism over logic.

_____

A friend of mine has two tickets in a corporate box at the England v Ireland rugby game on 18th March. He paid £300 each, but he didn't realise when he bought them months ago that it was going to be the same day as his wedding. If you are interested, he is looking for someone to take his place.

It's at the Dorchester Registry Office at 2.30pm.

_____

Someone stole my credit cards, but I didn't bother reporting it as the thief spends less than my wife.

_____

"It was love at first sight, Mrs Bennet, all her silly chatter and giggling, and the exquisite embroidery and scones."

I scared the postman today by going to the door completely naked.

I'm not sure what scared him more, my naked body or the fact that I knew where he lived.

_____

My wife and I went to the Royal Agricultural Show where she stopped at the bull pens. She stooped to read the sign at the prize-winner and pointed excitedly, "This bull won because it mated every day last year. You should find out what they fed him on."
I replied, "Whatever it was, I know it wasn't with the same cow."

I expect to make a full recovery and be discharged next week.

_____

I was broken-hearted when my girlfriend reported me to the police for stalking her.

But then, she wasn't really my girlfriend.

_____

A survey of middle-aged women has revealed that men do still have their uses:

Map reading, heavy shopping, furniture assembly, opening jars, and bedtime entertainment when the library is closed.

_____

We were so poor my father had to drive the car.

All versions of the Bible agree that at the time of Jesus' birth, Mary and Joseph were betrothed but not married, and this fact is the likely source of the 'birth in the stable' myth.

In an inept attempt to legitimise their marital status, the official announcement ended without the word 'relationship'.

––––––––––

Man: A simple organism that converts alcohol into urine.

Woman: A complex biological weapon hobbled by uncomfortable shoes.

––––––––––

Fort Trump will be the largest gated community in the world.

––––––––––

This may come as a surprise and disappointment to Wives and Women in general, but they are just about the last thing men think about.

Personally, I can't find anything of interest under X, Y and Z, and as it's a long way back to Beer and Cars most of us just hang around at S or W.

––––––––––

The Thought Police will never catch me, I don't think.

––––––––––

Never forget that when the government gives, it has first taken away, only more.

A drunk throws up over a sleeping dog outside the pub. The dog jumps up, shakes itself and runs off. The drunk turns to his mate and says,

"Jeez, I don't remember eating that."

_____

A car hit an elderly Jewish man and the paramedic asks him, "Are you comfortable?"

The man sighs, "I make a decent living."

_____

I just can't get a girlfriend even though I am fluent in English and Klingon.

_____

My wife keeps complaining I don't listen to her, or something like that.

_____

Air-kissing is just lips that pass in the night.

_____

"Knock, Knock."
"Who's there?"
"The Doctor."
"Doctor Who?"

"No, he's a fictional TV character who travels through space and time and won't be calling yesterday or tomorrow. I'm Doctor Strange, the psychiatrist come to treat your schizophrenia and socio-phobia."

"I'm not here until tomorrow, so bugger off, yesterday."

BARBER SHOP DUET

He: "Hi, how are you today?"
Me: "Nervous as hell."
He: "Why's that?"
Me: "Well, I have no idea what you are going to do to my hair. And since I have to take my glasses off for you, I can't see you or the mirror."
He: "OK, maybe I'll take mine off too to make you more comfortable. How much do you want off?"
Me: "A little bit all over, no cut off lines on the neck."
He: "So what style do you want?"
Me: "Give me a 'George Clooney'."
He: "Okay, then."

He then proceeded to give me the shortest haircut I had ever seen.

Me: "Hey, Clooney doesn't have a haircut like this."
He: Well, he damn well would have if he ever came in here, and anyway, not only are you getting a senior's discount, you won't need another trim for at least six months. That's a hell of a deal, for eleven bucks."
Me: "Maybe, but I could have had the shave for six."

———

When I walked out, I felt so naked that I'm sure everyone could see what I was thinking.

———

I once saw a wonderful topless ventriloquist, but I think her lips moved as well.

———

Don't wait for me. Godot.

HEARD ON THE RADIO

"Hello, you have reached 'RSNPB Men's Help Line.' My name is Bob. How can I help you, today?"

"Hi Bob, my name is Jack and I really need your advice on quite a serious problem.

"Hi, Jack, well what's the problem?"

"I have suspected for some time now that my wife has been cheating on me. You know, the usual signs, the phone rings and when I answer, the caller hangs up. Plus, she goes out with 'the girls' a lot, and with new revealing sexy outfits. I usually try to stay awake to look out for her when she comes home, but I always fall asleep. Anyway, last night about one o'clock, I woke up and she wasn't home. So, I hid in the garage behind my boat, left the up and over door open so I had a good view of the street, and waited for her. When she got home around three, she got out of a car, buttoned up her blouse, took her panties out of her purse and slipped them on. It was at that moment, while crouched behind the boat, that I noticed a hairline crack in the outboard motor mounting bracket. Is that something I can weld, or do I need to replace the whole bracket?"

———————

I just got back from a pleasure trip, taking the mother-in-law to the airport.

———————

Beer Belly 1: "Your round."
Beer Belly 2: "So are you, fat bastard!"

Doctor: "Mrs Cohen, your cheque has returned."
Mrs Cohen: "And so has my arthritis."

Judge: "You're in my court this morning for your uncontrolled drinking."
Drunk: "Well, let's get started then."

When I was growing up, we always had two choices for dinner – take it or leave it.

There is nothing more embarrassing than your mum going topless on holiday.

I haven't been back to Disneyland since.

It is mostly because of men that women dislike each other.

Tony: "I can do 100 press ups; what about you?"
Ron: "It depends who's underneath."

On my way home at the end of a tiring journey I spotted this poor old man staggering towards me.

That was when I walked straight into the shop window.

One should forgive one's enemies but remember the bastards' names.

FLOGGING A DEAD HORSE

A young man named Don bought a horse from a farmer for $200. The farmer agreed to deliver the horse later that day. However, the next day, the farmer drove up to Don's house and said,
"Sorry, but I have some bad news. The horse died."

Don: "Well, just give me my money back."
Farmer: "I'm afraid I've spent it already."
Don: "Ok then, bring me the dead horse."
Farmer: "What are going to do with a dead horse?"
Don: "I'm going to raffle him off."
Farmer: "You can't raffle off a dead horse!"
Don: "Sure I can. Watch me. I just won't tell anybody he's dead."

A month later, the farmer met up with Don and asked, "What happened with that dead horse?"
Don: "I raffled him off. I sold 500 tickets at five dollars apiece and made a profit of $2295."
Farmer: "Didn't anyone complain?"
Don: "Only the guy who won. So, I gave him his five dollars back."

Don is now rich and lives in Washington DC.

_____

Was there never a politician on a selfish mission?

_____

After suffering from depression for a while, the wife and I made a suicide pact last week.
Strangely once she went first, I began to feel a lot better, so I thought, "Sod it, I'll soldier on".

OLDIES

Old Dear 1: "I don't know what's going on in the world nowadays. If you had your time over again, would you change anything, everything?"

Old Dear 2: "I wouldn't get married, I know that."

Old Dear 1: "But wouldn't you want your children?"

Old Dear 2: "Of course, I would, just not those two."

———

Old Grumpy 1: "Good to see you, and in such good shape!"

Old Grumpy 2: "Well, I put that down to no longer drinking."

Old Grumpy 1: "Blimey, when did you stop that?"

Old Grumpy 2: "11:30 last night..."

———

Old Grumpy 1: "So, why's that glass in your hand?"

Old Grumpy 2: "Will power, sheer will power!"

———

Last summer I went to Tenerife and couldn't believe the number of tattoos and beer bellies I saw.
And the men were no better.

———

We were so poor I only had one wheel on my bicycle.

I woke up this morning at 9:30 sensing something was wrong. I got downstairs and found the wife face down on the kitchen floor, barely breathing. I panicked, I just didn't know what to do.

And then I remembered, the local café serves breakfast until 10:30.

———————

Charles Dickens came from a family of Somerset cider makers, and during his school holidays honed his writing skills coming up with slogans to promote sales of his uncle's products. It is believed he reinvented the drink as scrumpy to rhyme with pumpy and rumpy. But his most successful effort was the slogan that quickly quadrupled sales:

"She loves to start the day with a Dickens Cider."

———————

The undertaker turned up late for his funeral.
Fortunately, his partner was there, dead on time.

———————

CHINESE PROVERBS

Beware of barber with bald head.
Beware of plumber with wet overalls.
Beware of decorator with multi-coloured overalls.
Beware of electrician with shocking hair.
Beware of politician with open mouth.

———————

I spent three hours defrosting the fridge last night, or foreplay as she likes to call it.

The way into a man's heart is through his pyjamas.

———————

Two wrongs don't make a right, but they do make an excuse.

———————

I was puzzled why the brick was getting larger, and then it struck me…

———————

He was exposed for being too big for his pants.

———————

Your sole purpose in life may be simply to serve as a warning to others.

———————

After a long day holed up in their hide, the two ornithologists were back at their digs enjoying a quiet cup of Assam tea and swapping observation notes, when suddenly the door to their room flew off its hinges and the opening filled by the overbearing figure of their landlady holding her woodman's axe and her dead canary.

It was Mrs Crabtree and she was in no mood for pleasantries.

———————

I'm not saying my wife is an old bag, but she has managed 25 cups of tea out of one.

———————

I find that reading takes my mind off myself.

AN IRISH LETTER

Dear Son,

Just a few lines to let you know I'm still alive. I'm writing this letter slowly because I know you can't read fast. We are all doing very well. You won't recognize the house when you get home since we have moved. Your dad read in the newspaper that most accidents happen within 20 miles of home, so we moved 30 miles away. I won't be able to send you the address because the last family that lived here took the house numbers when they moved so that they wouldn't have to change their address. Your father's got a really good job now with 200 men under him. He's cutting the grass at the cemetery. Your sister Mary had a baby this morning, but I haven't found out if it's a boy or a girl, so I don't know whether you are an auntie or an uncle. Your brother Tom is still in the army. He's only been there a short while and they've already made him a court martial! Your Uncle Patrick drowned last week in a vat of whiskey in the Dublin Distillery. Some of his workmates tried to save him but he fought them off bravely. They cremated him, and it took three days to put out the fire. I'm sorry to say that your stupid cousin Seamus was arrested while riding his bicycle last week. They are charging him with dope peddling. I went to the doctor on Thursday and your father went with me. The doctor put a small tube in my mouth and told me not to talk for ten minutes. Your father offered to buy it from him. The weather isn't bad here. It only rained twice this week, first for three days and then for four days. Monday was so windy one of the chickens laid the same egg four times. John locked his keys in the car yesterday. We were worried because it took him two hours to get me and your father out. Three of your friends went off a bridge in a pick-up truck. Ralph was driving. He rolled down the window and swam to safety. Your other two friends were in the back. They drowned because they couldn't get the windows up. There isn't much more news at this time. Not much has happened.

Your loving Mum.

PS. I was going to send you some money, but I had already sealed the envelope

———————

No one ever went broke underestimating the taste of the American public.

———————

Puritanism is that haunting fear that someone somewhere may be enjoying themselves.

———————

"I've finally learnt the art of throwing my voice," I heard my teapot say.

———————

"Knock, knock."
"Who's there?"
"Buzz."
"Buzz who?"

"Stop messing about, Neil, and let me in.

FROZEN IN TIME

Scientist 1: "I think I have detected an anomaly in the spacetime continuum that is unbelievable."

Scientist 2: "I hope you aren't going to bang on about Appleby's new refrigerator that keeps food fresh by making time stand still, are you?"

Scientist 1: "Well yes, but only because I couldn't help noticing that the door seal was loose, and leaking stopped time all over the floor. It has been doing it since yesterday, when my watch stopped and the traffic lights outside were on red all day. If we don't do something about it now, the whole world will come to a standstill and stop rotating. And if that happens, the galaxy and the universe will be next, and will cease to expand. And we will all be frozen in time."

Scientist 2: "But wait a minute, or should that be a year, or even longer, if time has stopped still, how can we be standing here talking about it now and forever? If the planet has stopped rotating, wouldn't we have noticed it?"

Scientist 1: "We certainly would, but fortunately, Appleby's refrigerator is only 99.9% efficient, so it doesn't totally stop time, it only slows it right down, and since everything is relevant to everything else, we don't notice what used to take a few minutes now takes a million years or more."

Scientist 2: "I'm not sure I agree with your hypothesis, since I had noticed that this conversation was getting a little tedious."

An English teacher wrote the following words on the blackboard and asked the students to punctuate it correctly:

Woman without her man is nothing

The men wrote: Woman, without her man, is nothing.

The women wrote: Woman: without her, man is nothing.

––––––––––

As a boy I recall, insurance salesmen never reached our front door, thanks to the accuracy of mother's Olympic javelin.

––––––––––

I have just finished writing my latest memoirs, entitled *An Insomniac's Dreams*.

––––––––––

My Grandad's tall stories haven't been the same since the operation to remove his anecdotes.

––––––––––

A man is a woman's best friend.
He will reassure her when she feels insecure and comfort her after a bad day.
He will inspire her to do things she never thought she could do; to live without fear and forget regret.
He will enable her to express her deepest emotions and give in to her most intimate desires.
He will make sure she always feels that she's the most beautiful woman in the room and will enable her to be confident, sexy, seductive, and invincible.
Sorry, that's wrong; it's wine that does all that.

I don't understand why alcoholics have a problem. I've given up drinking hundreds of times.

_____

Artificial Intelligence will never beat natural stupidity.

_____

MEN'S PROBLEMS

Yesterday I had an appointment to see the Doctor for a prostate examination, and the waiting room was filled with patients.

As I approached the receptionist's desk, I could see that she was a large unfriendly woman built like a Sumo wrestler.

I gave her my name, and in a very loud voice, she said,

"Oh yes, you have come about your impotence."

All the patients in the waiting room snapped their heads around to look at me, embarrassed but composed, and in an equally loud voice I replied,

"No, I've come about a sex change operation, but I don't want the Doctor who did yours."

_____

It's marriage that prevents men from going through life thinking they have no faults at all.

_____

Airport Security: "Do you have anything sharp on you?"
Weary Passenger: "Only my pen and sardonic wit."

A CHRISTMAS TALE

It was Christmas Eve, and snow lay all about under the clear starlit sky. Inside, the house was warm from the roaring log fire with sprigs of holly and mistletoe decorating the mantle-piece. The family dog lay stretched out asleep on the hearth rug. Only the clicking of Grandma's knitting needles broke the silence. Ten-year-old twins Polly and Sally closed the picture books with which they had become bored and nestled up to Grandma in her rocking chair.

"Tell us a story, Grandma," pleaded Polly.

"Please do, Grandma," echoed Sally.

"Alright," said the old lady putting down her knitting and wrapping her arms around the children, "which one would you like to hear – Cinderella, Little Red Riding Hood, Snow White or Hansel and Gretel – there are so many, and you have heard them all before, so many times?"

In unison, with wide eyes and sweet smiles they replied,

"Forget the fairy tales and tell us about the time you were a whore in Chicago."

———————

"Where's your Xmas spirit, you miserable sod?"
"Probably still being shared out by airport security staff."

———————

It might have been more considerate if a speech impediment had been called a 'lithp'.

DRESS CODE

A fleeing Taliban terrorist, desperate for water, was plodding through the mountains when he saw a figure far off across the valley. Hoping to find water, he hurried down the mountain, across the valley, and up the other side only to find a very frail little Jewish man standing at a small makeshift display rack, selling neckties.

The Taliban terrorist asked, "Do you have water?"

The old man replied, "I have no water. Would you like to buy a tie? They are only five dollars."

The Taliban shouted hysterically, "Idiot Infidel, I do not need such an overpriced western adornment. I don't want one and I spit on your ties. I need water!"

"Sorry, I have none, just ties – pure silk, and only five dollars."

"Pah! A curse on your ties! If I had the time and strength I would wrap one around your scrawny little neck and choke the life out of you, but I must conserve my energy and find water!"

"Okay," said the little old Jewish man. "It does not matter that you do not want to buy a tie from me, or that you hate me, threaten my life, and call me Infidel. I will show you that I am bigger than any of that. If you continue over that hill to the east for about two kilometres, you will find a restaurant. It has the finest food and all the ice-cold water you will need. Go in peace."

Cursing him again, the desperate Taliban staggered away over the hill.

Several hours later he crawled back, almost dead, and gasped, "They won't let me in without a tie."

―――

Tie seller, "I can let you have my last one, and it's only twenty dollars."

―――

My wife and I always hold hands because if I let go, she shops.

―――

Don't worry yourself to death.

The Church is here to help you.

―――

Someone left a note on my car windscreen that said, 'Parking Fine.'
That was an unexpected compliment.

―――

A man walks into a bar, has a few drinks, goes home and lives happily ever after his decree absolute.

―――

She: "Will you still love me when I'm old, fat and ugly?"
He: "I do."

A FLIGHT OF FANCY

A man boarded a plane at Heathrow heading for New York, and as he settled into his seat an attractive young woman sat down beside him.

"Hello, business trip or vacation?" he asked politely.

She turned, smiled and said, "Business. I'm going to the Women's Convention on Sexuality in New York."

He swallowed hard. Here was one of the most beautiful women he had ever seen, sitting next to him, and she was going to a meeting of nymphomaniacs?

Struggling to contain his excitement, and his rampant imagination, he asked, "What will you be doing there?"

She replied, "I'm giving a lecture that challenges some of the myths about male sexuality."

"Really", he smiled nervously, "And what are they?"

"Well," she explained, "one unsupported myth is that African-American men are the most well-endowed, when surveys have revealed it's actually the native American Indian.

Another popular myth is that the French are the best lovers, when it's the Greeks.

And, I have also found that lovers with the most enthusiasm and stamina are the Welsh."

Suddenly, she became uncomfortable and said, "I'm sorry, that's enough about me, tell me something about yourself. What's your name?"

"Tonto," he said. "Tonto Papadopoulos, but my friends call me Taff.

Presidents and Prime Ministers are the world's leading experts in faked sincerity.

If I'd known the taxi was going this way, I'd have made more sandwiches.

A mental patient assaulted the hospital laundry staff and escaped.

Tabloid headline: *Nut screws washers and bolts.*

A gentleman is a man who takes his weight on his elbows.

Psychiatrist: "I think your problem is low self-esteem, which is very common amongst losers."

Lots of people have no talent whatsoever, so you shouldn't get depressed about it.

A patient in the mental hospital would spend hours every day with his ear pressed against the wall.
The doctor finally decided to see what he was listening to, and so put his ear to the wall and listened too.

Hearing nothing, he turned to the patient and said:
"I don't hear anything."

The patient replied: "I know. It's been like that for months."

My wife pleaded with me for a whole week to let her go on a course for oppressed women.

My latest book is entitled *"How to delegate."*
Actually, my wife wrote it for me.

Marriage is a relationship in which one person is always right, and the other is never wrong.

- Bullet points are deadly.

I believed we should all pay our taxes with a smile, but when I tried they insisted on money.

After finishing his Graham Greene novel and despite his atheism, my friend Stephen felt compelled to find a priest and confess his rather excessive enjoyment of a recent period of dry weather.

There's nothing worse than a long-winded joke that ends with the punchline that you've just forgotten.

———————

Don't marry the person you want to live with, marry the one you cannot live without.

But whatever you do, you'll regret it later.

———————

Life's disappointments are harder to cope with if you don't know enough swear words.

———————

Patriotism is the last refuge of the politician.

———————

Laziness is the habit of resting before you get tired.

———————

Publisher: "It's a beautifully written and charming story that reflects our genteel times. However, I think perhaps you ought to consider your future readership and pep it up a little with some foul language, gratuitously graphic sex scenes, and one or two coach and horse chases, Miss Brontë."

———————

The NSA know what you are getting for Christmas, if the TSA don't get their hands on it first.

———————

For every complex problem there is an answer that is clear, simple, and invariably wrong.

I asked the porter where the Psychiatric Ward was. He said, "It's just round the bend."

———————

Two Jehovah Witnesses arrive at the Pearly Gates. God whispers to St Peter, "Shush, we're not in."

———————

Experience allows you to recognise a mistake when you make it again.

———————

PILLOW TALK

After a busy day I settled down in my seat for a quiet journey home. No sooner had the train left the station when the man beside me pulled out his mobile phone and started up,

"Hi darling, it's Jack, I'm on the train… yes, I know it's the 9.30 not the 6.30… but I had a long meeting… no, not with the bimbo from the typing pool, with the boss… no darling you're the only one in my life… yes, I'm sure, cross my heart… no, I'll make it up to you, Sweetie," etc. etc.

After half an hour or so of this, the young woman opposite, driven beyond endurance, leans over to him and says rather loudly,

"Jack, can you please turn that phone off and come back to bed."

———————

Time was when the silent majority actually kept quiet.

Those who can't laugh at themselves unwittingly leave the job to others.

––––––––––

You know you're getting old when people start telling you how young you look.

––––

You know you're getting old when you enjoy remembering things more than doing them.

––––––––––

It doesn't matter how often a married man changes his job, he still ends up with the same boss.

––––––––––

Savings will ease your way through life's difficulties, more easily still if your parents did it for you.

––––––––––

Wise men talk because they have something to say. Fools talk because they have to say something.

––––––––––

English is only my mother tongue because my father hardly got to speak.

––––––––––

When we were first married, the sex was great, all stockings, suspenders and latex basques.
And then out of the blue, she just stopped me wearing them.

––––––––––

I do wonder what people do all day in Heaven.

Problems cannot be solved by the same quality of thinking that created them.

I've been having real problems with nuisance calls recently, such as,
"I expected you home from the pub three hours ago!"

My girlfriend might be blonde and anorexic, but I've stuck with her through thick and thin.

On one issue at least, men and women do agree. They both distrust women.

My memory is so bad, I could plan my own surprise parties.

She: "You only ever want sex when you're drunk!"
He: "That's not true, sometimes I want a kebab."

I went into the Army Recruitment Centre and saw a sergeant in his camouflage fatigues at his desk, and looking over his shoulder at the wall said, "Is there anyone there?"

He said, "Ha-ha, we don't like smartarses in the Army."

I said, "Maybe you should have a couple of pencils behind your ears and a few post-it notes stuck over your stripes."

No animals were offended in the writing of this book.

_____

The sun is already half way through its lifespan of nine billion years, but it wasn't until six thousand years ago that Civilisation made a bit of a late start.

If humanity wants to be remembered in the *History of the Universe*, even if only as a footnote, we need to get our act together, today.

_____

History has shown that in the end the minority is always right.

_____

Democracy is the philosophy that the common people know what they want and deserve to get it, good and hard.

_____

I'm beginning to sound like one of those people who likes the sound of their own voice.

_____

A good sermon should have a good beginning and a good ending and as close together as possible.

_____

My final ambition is a solo ascent of Everest from where I plan to conduct mankind in an anthem to myself.

_____

Like Tony Blair, I have been wrestling with my legacy, not with any achievements in my life, but with what goes on my headstone.

Here are a few contenders that I have offered to all of those I expect will want to visit my grave each month:

- I wish I could go to more meetings.

- His last words were 'It's…

- He died with his socks on.

- God blessed him for his atheism.

- He was never late in his lifetime.

- He met his final deadline.

- The flowers need changing.

- There's a devil of a party down here.

- I should have written my own eulogy.

- Here lies the ego of a great man.

- The End

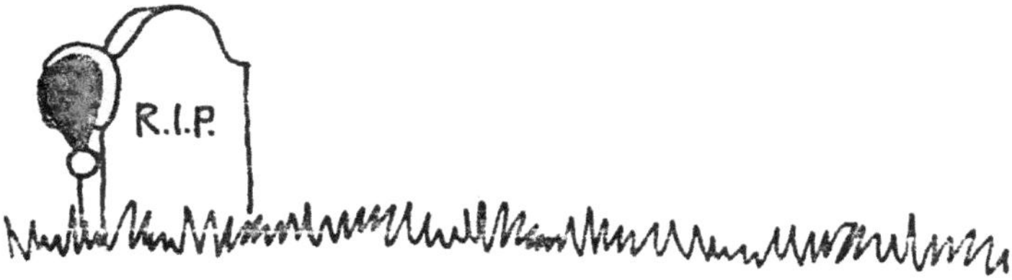
R.I.P.

ACKNOWLEDGEMENTS

I thank the following for their inspiration and contributions, and for their support which I now wear constantly:

Woody Allen
Steven Appleby
Glen Baxter
George Burns
Winston Churchill
Tommy Cooper
Les Dawson
Ken Dodd
Hreinn Friðfinnsson
Mel Hare
Tony Harrison
Ron Haslam
Bob Hope
Dyne Hudson
H. L. Mencken
P.J. O'Rourke
Monty Python
N-F Nielsen
Jack Ware
Oscar Wilde
Billy Wilder
Naomi Zawada

INDEX   Page

Blair, T.   101

ABOUT THE AUTHOR

Jack Idle was born in 1946 and lived in a mobile home parked on bricks at 66 Braehurst Road in Liverpool until it was demolished some thirty years later.

In 1977, his mother reported him missing together with his hedgehog Spike.

A woman who wishes to remain anonymous admitted she had been married to him until the evening he slipped down the back of the sofa. Despite an exhaustive search, she only found a remote control and an old hairbrush.

A planned feature film of his life was shelved when GCHQ denied access to their vast surveillance-video archive claiming that relevant footage was unsuitable for children or adults, and was dangerously dull.

Since 2000, he has only ventured outdoors in heavy disguise which he changes daily. His last confirmed sighting was in 1999, when he was captured on low-resolution footage whilst abandoning a half-filled trolley of pet food in a Bloomsbury supermarket.

He never returned to complete his purchase, and the pet food was also shelved.

He has written many best sellers using both his own and other authors' *noms de plume*, but this one is his final *opus magnum*, he told us.

He found his crayons yesterday.